TRUST YOUR CHILDREN

VOICES
AGAINST
CENSORSHIP
IN
CHILDREN'S
LITERATURE

BY
MARK I. WEST

D1293070

NEAL-SCHUMAN PUBLISHERS
NEW YORK   LONDON

Published by Neal-Schuman Publishers, Inc.
23 Leonard Street
New York, NY 10013

Printed and bound in the United States of America.

Library of Congress Cataloging-in-Publication Data

West, Mark I.
  Trust your children.

  Bibliography: p.
  1. Children—Books and reading.   2. Children's
literature—Censorship—United States.   3. Censorship—
United States.   I. Title.
Z1037.A1W38   1988   363.3'1   87-31452
ISBN 1-55570-021-7

To Norma Klein, who helped pave my way,
and
Nancy Northcott, who tried not to divert me.

Contents

Foreword

Reading has become controversial in America. In one midwestern town, the school board scoured its card catalog and righteously banned *Making It with Mademoiselle*. They were forced to put it back on the shelves when they discovered it was a how-to book on sewing, published for teenagers by *Mademoiselle* magazine. In North Carolina there was an objection to J.D. Salinger's *Catcher in the Rye*. This may have originated with the critic's misreading of the title which he thought was *Catch Her in the Rye*.

Even encyclopedias are suspect, for which we now have written instructions on how to clean them up. In the publication *Christian School Builder,* the following suggestions were offered:

> (In encyclopedias) we are not battling a plot that captivates minds but are looking for erroneous information, sensual pictures, and unchaste details. . . . One of the areas that needs correction is immodesty due to nakedness and posture. This can be corrected by drawing clothes on the figures or blotting out entire pictures with a magic marker. This needs to be done with care as the magic marker can be erased from the glossy paper used in printing encyclopedias.
>
> You can overcome this by taking a razor blade and lightly scraping the surface until it loses its glaze. After this is done the magic marker will not erase. (As for evolution) . . . cutting out the sections (on the subject) is practical if the portions removed are not thick enough to cause damage to the spine of the book as it is opened and closed in normal use. When the sections needing correction are too thick, paste together being careful not to smear portions of the book not intended for correction.

Education is more than an abstract issue of public policy; education shapes our own future, our children's future, and the future of our entire society. Without reading there can be no education.

With *Trust Your Children*, Mark I. West has provided parents, teachers, and citizens with a powerful primer on the importance of reading and literature for the next generation of Americans.

For the past seven years as President of People for the American Way I have had the opportunity to learn about what is going on in hundreds of school systems across the country. I have followed the activities of those who would like to censor public school textbooks and curricula; I have spoken with courageous teachers, librarians, and administrators who have resisted the censors; and we've evaluated textbooks in subjects ranging from civics to biology to history.

Initially, I was concerned about the censorship of textbooks and curricula because I saw it primarily as a constitutional liberties issue. Now I'm concerned because censorship may prevent the next generation, including my children, from getting the quality of education I was privileged to receive.

My own experience leads me to these five conclusions. *The future of education in America rests with the future of public education.* Not only because more than 85 percent of our young people are enrolled in the public schools, but also because the public schools are best suited for bringing together young people from every background and instilling in them a sense of our common culture, our common heritage, and our common destiny.

Our schools must link the goals of equality and excellence. In the final analysis, these goals don't conflict with each other— they reinforce each other. We owe our young people, all our young people, nothing less than to demand the best of them and to give all of them the opportunity to be their best. We cheat every student we write off; we cheat every student we talk down to; we cheat every student whom we promote or graduate for no reason except that he or she kept a seat warm.

Our schools must do more than convey a set of facts or even a set of basic skills. They must, above all, teach young people how to think. The basic process of thinking—critical thinking, analytical thinking, disciplined thinking—is at the heart of every other skill students learn in school, from solving mathematical problems, to conducting scientific experiments, to appreciating a work of literature, to writing a persuasive essay.

In order to learn how to think, students must have something to think about. That means, when it comes to curricula, more is better. Students should be exposed to scientific theories, literary classics, and the study of history, including its proudest chapters as well as its most tragic and shameful ones. I am more concerned about students who have been exposed to too few of the important things than those who may have been exposed to too many difficult and disturbing things.

And, most important, *education should be governed by standards of excellence, not orthodoxy, timidity, or intolerance.* There are those who would protect our students from studying scientific theories like evolution, reading literary classics like *Romeo and Juliet,* or learning about tragic chapters of history like the Holocaust. Those who would restrict teachers' lesson plans and students' reading lists are doing something even worse than denying young people information; they are preventing them from learning to think for themselves. A growing mind must be encouraged, not shackled.

I'm convinced that today's generation of young people need the same advantage I had a quarter of a century ago: a renewed national concern with excellence in education. We are living in a time similar to the late fifties and early sixties. Three decades ago, Sputnik punched a hole in America's complacency. We took a hard look at our standards in the world.

The result was a series of critical studies of our schools; a much-needed infusion of funds; and a greater emphasis upon excellence, especially in science and math.

Today, Americans are more concerned with economic competition than with the space race and the missile gap; we're looking anxiously over our shoulders at Japan, not Russia. However, I think we have the same kind of concern about the decline in our skills and our schools that jolted us into action in the post-Sputnik era.

A series of national commissions and well-publicized reports have alerted us to the deterioration of textbooks, teaching, and test scores. Americans have responded to the alarm: secretaries of education, governors and chief state school officers, the news media, teachers unions, the business community, and parents and taxpayers. Indeed, there's a good reason to believe the late 1980s will be remembered as an era of educational excellence.

This is the good news. Once again, Americans are concerned about education. The bad news is that there is a lot to be concerned about. In fact, for those of us who follow education, the news keeps getting worse. Just over a year ago, a report concluded American elementary school children trail well behind their Japanese and Chinese counterparts in academic achievement scores, particularly in math and science. Another study found most students can't express themselves effectively in writing. And still another study found only a small percentage of our young people can reason effectively about what they are reading and writing.

Interestingly enough, none of these indicators measures how many facts our students have memorized. They measure basic intellectual skills—the abilities to solve mathematical problems, write effectively, and understand what one is reading. In short, our young people are flunking basic mental fitness.

Three decades ago there was a best seller called *Why*

Johnny Can't Read. This year, a study of what's wrong with our schools might be entitled *Why Johnny—and Janey—Can't Think*. Here's one reason why Johnny and Janey can't think: because there are well-organized activists in this country who don't want our young people to read about, much less think about, subjects ranging from human biology to evolution to the Holocaust. Censorship is a national epidemic that is afflicting every part of the country—not only rural communities in the South and the Midwest, but virtually every major metropolitan area throughout the nation.

And, most alarmingly of all, the censors are no longer targeting individual books. They are trying to eliminate any mention of entire subjects and even courses of study. The following are examples of how censors are gutting our children's education—examples which I have drawn from studies of major publishers' high school textbooks.

- Because of the censors' holy war against evolution, half of the biology textbooks don't cover evolution adequately, and one-sixth don't mention evolution at all.
- Because of the censors' fixation on a few common words in novels, one major Boston publisher has even started removing words from the dictionary.
- Because the censors have made them jittery about covering troublesome issues, civics textbooks fail to devote adequate coverage to important controversies of recent years, such as Watergate and the Vietnam War.
- Because so many censors object to discussing moral and civic values and promoting positive behavior patterns—unless this discussion is framed in sectarian religious terms—they have pressured many school systems to stop offering programs to discourage drug and alcohol abuse, teenage pregnancy, and teen suicide.
- And, largely because the censors have made religious beliefs controversial, history textbooks fail to cover the enormous contributions that a diversity of religious groups have made to our society.

Not all censorship comes from the Right. A few years ago the Berkeley, California, school board banned a book because they thought it was too anti-Soviet. And there are well-meaning people who want to protect young people from reading *Huckleberry Finn* and *The Merchant of Venice.*

The fact is, however, most censorship activity comes from organizations connected with the Religious Right: Pat Robertson's Grassroots Network; Jerry Falwell's Moral Majority; Phyllis Schlafly's Eagle Forum; and a couple in Texas, Mel and Norma Gabler, who run a sort of anti-think tank for all the others. Here is Pat Robertson's view of our public education system:

> The state steadily is attempting to do something that few states other than the Nazis and the Soviets have attempted to do, namely, to take the children away from the parents and to educate them in a philosophy that is amoral, anti-Christian, and humanistic and to show them a collectivist philosophy that will ultimately lead toward Marxism, Socialism and a Communistic type of ideology.

Tim LaHaye, who is the President of the American Coalition for Traditional Values, has declared, "Modern public school education is the most dangerous single force in a child's life." Jerry Falwell has written in his book *Listen America,* "I hope to live to see the day when there are no more public schools. The churches will have them taken over and the Christians will be running them."

The Religious Right has made headlines by successfully moving from the classrooms to the courtrooms. They have won federal district court cases in Tennessee and Alabama that have granted official sanction to one of their craziest—and most dangerous—doctrines. It is a doctrine that seeks to protect their children, and ultimately all children, from being exposed to ideas with which they disagree. Their argument can be boiled down to this: That unless our public schools teach their religious dogma, we are undermining the religious faith of their children, and violating their constitutional rights.

In Tennessee, Rev. LaHaye and his wife won the right for students not to come into contact with ideas other than their own. Their objections included not simply *The Diary of Anne Frank* and the *Wizard of Oz,* but a short story about New Mexico, because it discusses Catholic religious observance. Vicki Frost, the lead plaintiff, summed it up when she said that we cannot be tolerant in that we accept other religious views on an equal basis as our own. Even the Tennessee curriculum on world pollution came under attack.

In Alabama, Pat Robertson won official judicial recognition for a conspiracy theory they've promoted for years: the idea that a godless religion called "secular humanism" dominates the public schools. Pat Robertson was appointed chief curriculum supervisor for Alabama schools by Judge Hand. Fortunately, the Circuit Courts of Appeals have reversed these two rulings, but Robertson and LaHaye have vowed to fight on to the Supreme Court.

Trust Your Children comes at a most opportune time, just as the censors have lost important battles in court. Many will be inclined to say the problem has therefore gone away. But, as this volume attests, the wave of censorship activity has not yet crested. The freedom to read may be protected in the courtroom but it will continue to be under assault in classrooms, libraries, and publishing houses.

Through revealing interviews with authors, experts, and litigators, Mark West brings alive the drama of the daily struggle of some people to dictate what others may read. West is not a neutral observer. He stands in contrast to a television network interviewer who, a few years ago, presided over a debate between a book burner and an advocate of the freedom to read and concluded the argument by wishing both sides the best of luck. West is a passionate advocate of teaching our children to confront the real world as it is—of trusting our children. This book should be required reading by any school board member, librarian, teacher, or publisher who is ever inclined to do otherwise.

Anthony T. Podesta
Founding President of
People for the American Way

Preface

Children's literature has always been subjected to censorship, but prior to the 1970s most censorship activity took place in an author's study or an editor's office. Authors from the 1940s or 1950s, for example, knew that if they wanted to write for children they needed to uphold a whole gamut of taboos. They accepted as a given that they could not use swear words, make references to sexuality, or address controversial social problems. By accepting these restrictions, they became their own censors. If they deliberately or unwittingly violated one of these taboos, their editors would strongly recommend revising the offending passage. Occasionally, of course, children's books were published that violated a taboo or two, and some of these books were attacked by parents and banned from libraries. For the most part, however, the censorship of children's books occurred before they saw print.

This pattern continued well into the 1960s, but it began to break down toward the end of the decade. During this period, a number of children's authors, editors, and publishers started ignoring some of the taboos that had restricted children's literature for so many years. As a result, a new breed of children's books came into being. These books dealt with such topics as menstruation, masturbation, divorce, drug abuse, and racism.

At first these books aroused little controversy, but during the second half of the 1970s several of them came under attack. Some irate parents began demanding that many of these books be banned from school and public libraries, and several conservative political and religious organizations launched campaigns against a number of books. They also attacked textbooks and put pressure on book clubs not to market certain titles. This trend accelerated dramatically in the early 1980s, and it shows no signs of abating in the near future. Overt censorship has emerged as a major problem in the field of children's literature.

Numerous authors, civil libertarians, librarians, and scholars view this problem as a serious threat to Americans' freedom of expression, and some have strongly argued that the First Amendment should apply to children's literature as well as to literature intended for adults. In addition to sparking a debate over the freedom of expression, the censorship of children's literature has brought another important issue to the surface. The children's authors whose works are being banned generally hold different beliefs about childhood than do the proponents of censorship. Thus, on one level, this censorship debate is also a debate about the psychology of children.

While the censorship of children's literature has attracted the attention of the news media, most of the coverage has been somewhat superficial. A typical news story begins with a quotation from a parent who claims that an "immoral" children's book should be removed from the library and closes with a quotation from a free-speech advocate who argues that banning the book would curtail the intellectual freedom of children. The rest of the story is filled with the facts surrounding the case. Generally, however, there is little analysis of the conflicting child-rearing beliefs of the censored author and the offended parent.

In order to understand why children's literature has become such a battleground, it is necessary to examine these beliefs. *Trust Your Children* provides several authors, publishers, and anticensorship activists with a forum to express their beliefs about childhood, parenting, and children's literature in addition to giving them an opportunity to explain why they object to censorship.

Of the eighteen interviewees, ten are authors, three

are publishers, and five are anticensorship activists. Although all the authors have had their books censored, there are significant differences among their books. Judy Blume and Norma Klein write realistic books about relationships and family life, while Robert Cormier's books generally deal with an adolescent's confrontations with society. Betty Miles also writes about societal issues, but her books usually focus on preadolescents. Harry Mazer's and Nat Hentoff's books tend to be about the experiences of adolescent boys who are beginning to break away from home. Roald Dahl is the author of many humorous fantasy stories, while Daniel Keyes is most famous for his science fiction novel, *Flowers for Algernon*. The final two authors, Maurice Sendak and John Steptoe, are known for their picture books.

Richard Jackson, Phyllis Fogelman, and Stephen Roxburgh all have published children's books that have been targeted by censors. The remaining interviewees are either affiliated with anticensorship organizations or have engaged in anticensorship work. Judith Krug directs the American Library Association's Office for Intellectual Freedom, Leanne Katz directs the National Coalition Against Censorship, Barbara Parker worked for People for the American Way, and Amy McClure has ties with the Children's Literature Association. The final interview is with Timothy Dyk, a lawyer who specializes in First Amendment issues.

As its title implies, *Trust Your Children* is deliberately one-sided. I hope, however, that what this book lacks in breadth it makes up for in depth. I should also make it clear from the beginning that I did not conduct these interviews from a neutral stance. I strongly oppose all forms of censorship, and I offer this book as my contribution to the anticensorship movement.

Mark I. West

Acknowledgments

If it were not for the cooperation of a number of people, this book would never have progressed beyond the idea stage. I owe my greatest debt to the eighteen people who agreed to be interviewed. Not only did they take time out of busy schedules to talk with me, but they went out of their way to make me feel welcome. I especially want to thank Norma Klein for being so helpful.

This project involved a lot of traveling, and some of my travel expenses came out of funds provided by the Foundation of the University of North Carolina at Charlotte and from the state of North Carolina. Several friends put me up while I was away from home, including James Riemer, James and Peg Fry, and Herb and Florence Greenberg. Their hospitality was much appreciated.

The English Department at the University of North Carolina at Charlotte awarded me a teaching reduction to work on this book, and for this I am grateful. My gratitude also goes to Stephen Doheny-Farina and Robin Hemley, two of my colleagues in the department, for their encouragement. I also want to thank Eleanor Stafford, one of the department's secretaries, for typing the final manuscript.

Finally, I want to express my appreciation to Nancy Northcott for being so supportive of this project. She deserves a medal for listening so patiently while I complained about transcribing.

Photos and Photo Credits

Judy Blume by Thomas Victor, page 2
Norma Klein by Thomas Victor, page 16
Robert Cormier by Finkle Photographer, page 28
Betty Miles by Matt Miles, page 38
Harry Mazer by Mimi Cataldo, page 52
Nat Hentoff, page 60
Roald Dahl, page 70
Daniel Keyes by Harry Snavely, page 78
Maurice Sendak by Candid Lang, page 86
John Steptoe, page 92
Richard Jackson, page 100
Phyllis J. Fogelman by Frannie Chisolm, page 108
Stephen Roxburgh by Miriam Cooper, page 116
Judith F. Krug, page 124
Leanne Katz, page 134
Barbara Parker by Joan Marcus, page 144
Amy A. McClure, page 154
Timothy B. Dyk, page 164

THE
AUTHORS
SPEAK

Judy Blume

When Judy Blume began writing children's books in the late 1960s, no one would have guessed that she was destined to become the most frequently censored author in the history of American children's literature. Her first book, *The One in the Middle Is the Green Kangaroo* (1969), did not violate any taboos. Although her second book, *Iggie's House* (1970), dealt with racism, it also fit fairly neatly within the framework of conventional children's literature. It was not until the publication of her third book, *Are You There God? It's Me, Margaret* (1970), that Blume began breaking new ground, for *Margaret* was one of the first children's books to contain a straightforward discussion of menstruation and breast development. The book quickly achieved best-seller status and established Blume as a major figure in children's literature.

Blume went on to write a number of other innovative children's books in which she dealt with such sensitive subjects as masturbation, sexual intercourse, neglective parents, and cruel children. None of her books sparked much controversy until the late 1970s. Since then, however, her books have come under frequent attack. During the first half of the 1980s, over sixty attempts to ban Blume's books were reported to the *Newsletter on Intellectual Freedom* (published by the Office for Intellectual Freedom, American Library Association), and it is estimated that many more attempts went unreported. The censors have focused their attacks on five of Blume's books: *Margaret, Then Again, Maybe I Won't* (1971), *Deenie* (1973), *Blubber* (1974), and *Forever* (1975).

Your first two books, *The One in the Middle Is the Green Kangaroo* and *Iggie's House*, seem more traditional than most of your other children's books. Did you approach the writing of them with a different attitude?

When I wrote *Green Kangaroo* and *Iggie's House*, I wanted work and I was learning. But I knew that they didn't come from inside. After they were done, I said to myself, "Now that I've figured out how to write books I'm going to write what I know to be true." That's when I wrote *Are You There God? It's Me, Margaret.*

In *Margaret* you wrote about menstruation, breast development, and other subjects that most children's authors who wrote before you had never ever mentioned. Was this an act of courage?

It was not courage. It was naiveté. I had absolutely no idea I was writing a controversial book. There was nothing in it that wasn't a part of my sixth grade experience. For six months of my life I was possessed by the idea of menstruation and breast development. But I wasn't the only one. My friends were equally possessed. We talked about it endlessly just as Margaret and her friends do in the book. The book comes right out of my own childhood experiences.

Why do you suppose other authors had not written books similar to *Margaret* in the fifties and sixties?

I'm not sure, but I can tell you this much. When I started out, I took a writing course. I loved my teacher, Lee Wyndham. She was a children's writer during the late forties and fifties, and she gave me my first professional encouragement. But she lectured to us each week, and she had absolute rules and regulations for writing children's books. She had a whole list of things under "Thou Shalt Not." I don't know if she ever mentioned sexuality, but I remember her saying, for example, a child must never eavesdrop. There were all of these incredible rules, and maybe people believed them. Maybe they felt that they couldn't get anything published if they didn't.

Why did you feel free to break the rules?

I remember saying to myself, "Never mind these rules. This isn't what it's really like." I guess I knew that I was breaking rules, but I didn't do it in any kind of hostile or rebellious way. I was just determined to write about what I remembered.

When Lee saw the manuscript to *Margaret,* she wrote me a long letter about it. She said, "Goodness, what's all this napkin practice doing in here." However, she was also the first to write to congratulate me when *The New York Times* gave it a good review.

Did you have any trouble finding a publisher for *Margaret?*

I was very fortunate. While I was writing *Iggie's House,* I came across an announcement in a magazine that a new publishing company was interested in realistic books about childhood, especially the middle years. I contacted them and met Dick Jackson and Bob Verrone. They were young, and they had just started Bradbury Press. They accepted *Iggie's House* and after that, *Margaret.* I didn't know it then, but now I understand that they took a big chance on me.

I have always had the happiest publishing experiences with Bradbury. If I could work with Dick Jackson on every book, I would. I miss him a lot because I have not done a book with him since *Tiger Eyes*. He taught me everything I know about revising. From years of working with him, I was able to rewrite my adult books on my own. It was as if he were right behind me asking questions.

Do you think that an established press would have accepted *Margaret*?

Harper and Row might have taken it. They published Louise Fitzhugh, and she was my idol. I loved her book *Harriet the Spy*.

Were there any other authors that you emulated when you were starting out?

Elaine Konigsburg had just published *Jennifer, Hecate, Macbeth, William McKinley, and Me, Elizabeth,* and I thought that was the most wonderful book. The kids in that book were real. I also loved Beverly Cleary's books. They were delightful and funny. I wanted to write books like those.

Do you remember the first time one of your books was censored?

It goes back to my children's elementary school principal. I gave the school some copies of *Margaret* when it first came out, but he refused to allow the books in the school's library. Still, I didn't pay too much attention. I just thought that he was a nut. It never occurred to me that it was going to happen again.

Also, there was a woman who called me up right after *Margaret* came out and asked me if I had written it. When I said I had, she called me a Communist and hung up.

I recently found out that in the beginning my publishers tried to protect me from the controversy. I never saw the letters or heard about the phone calls. I guess they thought, "Why should we worry her?" Of course, that was wrong. I should always have known.

At what point did you begin to view the censorship of your books as a serious problem?

It wasn't until 1980. The big surge in censorship came right after Reagan was elected. The reported cases quadrupled overnight.

Have your books been subjected to forms of censorship other than being banned from libraries?

I have received numerous letters about censorship in classrooms. Some teachers tell their students, "If you read books by Judy Blume for your book report, you automatically get ten points taken off your grade." I heard about one seventh grade teacher who told her students that my books are garbage, teenage trash, pornography.

Do you ever get angry letters from children?

One of the most painful letters I ever got from a child was addressed to "Jewdy Blume." It was from a nine-year old child. She called me Jewdy all the way through and underlined in crayon the letters J E W over and over. The letter was about

Starring Sally J. Freedman as Herself, and it said that I had a lot of nerve making Jewish angels. It was very anti-Semitic, and it floored me. I'm used to objections to sex and language, but that kind of feeling and hate from a young child was very frightening.

What are your reactions to the well-publicized case in Peoria where three of your books were banned by the school district?

The good thing about all of that publicity is that it made more people aware of the problem of censorship. Also, since school districts don't want that kind of publicity, others might be more hesitant to ban books. Actually, what happened in Peoria wasn't all that unusual. I think the reason that the media jumped on the bandwagon is that it happened during the same week that I got an intellectual freedom award. The media blows things up, but every now and then they come through in helping people to become more aware, so I try not to judge them.

Has the increase in censorship activity affected the marketing of children's books?

Yes, it is getting so that children's books that deal with the nitty-gritty side of life are being published as adult books or young adult books. I'm still angry with Bradbury Press for advertising *Forever* as my first book for adults. It wasn't for adults, but that was their way of protecting themselves and, I guess, me. Also, that was before the term "young adult book" was widely used. Today, *Forever* would be published as a young adult book.

Who defends your books when they come under attack?

It is usually a teacher, librarian, concerned citizen, or the kids themselves. In Peoria it was a parent. In Loveland, Colorado, it was the kids, but I'm sure that they were backed by supportive adults. The reading public has to be encouraged to take a stand and defend the books that they want to read. It is not the author's job to come forward and become defensive. I try to be supportive and encouraging to all those who care enough to defend my books. If I went around the country trying to defend my books and other books under attack, I would never have the time to write another.

Do you think that a new author who wrote children's books such as yours would have an easier time getting published now than when you started to write?

They would have a harder time right now. I was unknowingly lucky because I came around at the right time, and it worked. I think that it is much, much tougher today.

It is even tougher for me. I'll tell you a story about *Tiger Eyes* that I am ashamed of. At one point Davey, the fifteen-year-old girl in the book, goes out to her first social event since her father was killed, and that night she masturbates for the first time since his death. It was an emotional release. She felt alive again. There was just one line in the book, but my publishers said that it would make the book controversial and limit the book's audience. I took it out, but I wish that I hadn't. If all of us who write begin to worry about censorship, it is our readers who are going to wind up losing.

The controversy surrounding the few references to masturbation in *Deenie* suggests that book censors find this topic especially alarming. Do you think that this is true?

Masturbation seems to be less acceptable than intercourse in books for young people. *Deenie* always gets in trouble because of female masturbation. I once met a school librarian who told me that the male principal of her school would not let her put *Deenie* in the library because Deenie masturbated. He said it would be different if it were a boy.

Is it more acceptable to write about boys' sexuality?

I'm not sure that's true. If a boy character masturbates, many female librarians become terrified.

Why do some adults find it nearly impossible to accept children's sexuality?

I think that adults are so uncomfortable about their own sexuality that they can't begin to deal with their children's. They are afraid that their children will ask them questions about sex and not only will they feel embarrassed and uneasy but they won't know the answers either. I once interviewed a group of men, and I asked them what a uterus is. Not one of them could say a uterus is . . . . Many parents don't have the answer, and this makes them feel ashamed.

Most parents grew up without ever talking about sex. The message that they got from their parents was, "We don't talk about sex in our family. It isn't something good or something we enjoy." This pattern continues for generation after generation unless somebody breaks it, and for many families it remains unbroken. I know this from the letters I receive from children all over the country.

When I spoke at the American Psychiatric Association convention a child psychiatrist who was sitting at my dinner table turned to me and said, "Come on, all parents today are open with their children about sex." Because he lives in a liberal university town, he really didn't know that this is not the way it is everywhere. I could not believe how naive he was.

Would you say that adult fears about sexuality are the major reason your books are so controversial?

Yes, and the fact that my books are popular among children. Adults have always been suspicious of books that kids like. It seems as if some adults choose to forget what mattered to them when they were children. If they remembered, they might not have this warped view of what's "good" for kids. So many of our children's librarians tell kids, "I want you to read *these* books, not those books that you like. Those books that you like are no good for you." I find that if kids like something, many adults automatically assume that it is harmful. Many adults do not trust children.

***Blubber* is one of your books that is frequently targeted by censors, but it contains no sexual passages. The reason it gets in trouble is that the child characters are not portrayed as innocent and happy. How do you feel about the notion of childhood innocence?**

I don't know what childhood innocence is supposed to mean. Children are inexperienced, but they are not innocent.

Feelings of jealousy and anger begin early. Children have little control over their lives, and this causes both anger and unhappiness. Childhood can be a terrible time of life. No kid wants to stay a kid. It is only adults who have forgotten who say, "If only I could be a kid again." The fantasy of childhood is to *be* an adult.

What do you say to people who argue that children are naturally happy?

I think they have forgotten what it's like to be young. What children have to face out there can be so hard. They have to learn to cope with situations they didn't create. Many of the letters I get from young kids deal with life in school and life with friends, and they tell how incredibly painful every day can be. Unhappiness does not come from books; it comes from life.

How do you feel when people say that your books let children in on adult secrets?

Secrets, secrets! I grew up hating secrets, and I still hate secrets. I cannot stand the idea that anyone has a secret from me. Tell me anything. I don't care how bad it is, but don't keep it a secret. I think most kids would agree with me. Like all age groups, they want people to be honest with them.

What motivates parents to censor their children's reading materials?

Some parents are frightened by the idea of exposing their children to new ideas, ideas that are different from their own.

Some parents like to say, "This is what's right, and that's it." It is much harder to listen to what your child says than it is to set down rules. Censorship grows out of fear. There is a tremendous amount of fear on the part of parents. I don't want to go on any crusades, but if I could do something, I would like to help parents learn to be less afraid and to trust themselves and their children more. Fear comes from insecurity. None of us knows how to raise kids. What experience do we have? We learn as we go.

When children are young, parents feel that they can control them, and they can to a certain extent. But as children grow, parents have to learn to give up some of that control, and that is what they find terrifying. These parents fear the outside world; they fear the influence of the world on their children. They want to control so tightly that they constantly feel threatened. One way of controlling is to censor books and movies.

Have you had any encounters with this type of parent?

My most recent encounter was at a talk that I gave. When it was time to take questions, a woman who has a seven-year-old child spoke up, and she went on and on. She wanted warnings printed on books that would say, "This isn't suitable for seven-year-olds." She was very angry at me because my books are for all ages, and she thought that I had betrayed her. I asked her what she was afraid of, but she couldn't answer. She just kept getting angrier and angrier. In the end, she never could tell me what she was so afraid of because I don't think she knew. I think that she just wants to protect her little child from the world.

Now, I have read a lot of books that are not for seven-year-olds, and I can understand parents' concerns. But parents have to ask themselves, "So what if my kid browses through the books at the library and picks up a book for older kids or even adults. What can happen?" The kid might ask a question, and if he does, I say answer him.

I could show you letter after letter from parents who say, "I want to be the one to decide when to tell my kid about sex." Well, that's fine with me, but I hope they don't wait forever. I'm afraid that these parents will never answer their children's questions about sex. Their problem is not just with sex, though. It's with death. It's with money. It's with feelings and emotions, everything that is most important in life. Some people do not know how to talk to kids about anything personal, anything tough. Kids learn about life from us. Part of our responsibility, as parents, is to give them the tools which will enable them to make wise decisions and become responsible, caring adults.

Norma Klein

Norma Klein has a lot in common with Judy Blume. They were both born in 1938, they both grew up around New York City, they both became popular children's authors during the 1970s, and they both know what it is like to have their books banned. Klein published her first children's book, *Mom, the Wolf Man and Me,* in 1972. The book soon attracted attention, in part, because its main character is the daughter of an unmarried woman. Klein has gone on to write over twenty-five children's books, many of which deal with childhood sexuality, nontraditional families, and other sensitive subjects.

While Klein's candidness has always met with a certain amount of parental disapproval, the controversy surrounding her books has significantly intensified since 1980. A number of her books have been the focus of censorship attempts. Book censors have attacked *It's Not What You Expect* (1973) for containing a character who has an abortion, *Naomi in the Middle* (1974) for explaining how conception occurs, *It's Okay If You Don't Love Me* (1977) for implying that teenage girls may want to engage in sexual relationships, and *Breaking Up* (1980) for portraying a lesbian mother in a positive light. In fact, a survey of the censorship cases reported in the *Newsletter on Intellectual Freedom* (published by the Office for Intellectual Freedom, American Library Association) revealed that the only children's author who has had more titles banned than Klein is Blume.

What led you to begin writing children's books that dealt with sexuality, divorce, and other subjects that had previously been ignored by children's authors?

I came to it rather innocently as did Judy Blume, Robert Cormier, and several other authors who are now considered controversial. Although we came from different backgrounds, we had certain points in common. We had been children in the forties and fifties, and we had found very little that was good to read in the way of realistic fiction for children. We mainly read idealized, sanitized, sentimentalized books. Often we rushed into adult fiction at eleven or twelve.

As we had children of our own and started buying books for them, we began saying, "My God, this is 1970 and it's the same thing." People were talking about kids being turned off reading because of television, but I felt that a lot of them were being turned off because there wasn't much to read that wasn't pap, that wasn't condescending. I thought that kids needed an alternative. That helped motivate me to start writing for them after ten years of publishing short stories for adults.

Was there anything about your background that predisposed you to write nontraditional children's books?

I think it's significant that Judy Blume and I, two of the children's book authors most frequently attacked for our openness, are both Jewish. American Jewish authors have often been more irreverent and iconoclastic. Erica Jong and Philip Roth are just two examples out of many. But the children's book world has always been made nervous by this irreverence. I remember reading books in my childhood about kids playing on grandmother's farm and wives polishing silver napkin rings. The fathers wore cowboy hats, and the mothers wore little flowered aprons. I grew up as a New York Jew, and nobody I knew was like that. When I read these books I thought, "That's not my world."

My husband is not Jewish, and often when I describe to him a book I'm planning to write, he feels I'm deliberately flouting convention. But I wasn't brought up to regard all conventions as sacred. I'm not a rebel, trying to stir things up just to be provocative. I'm doing it because I feel like writing about what I see as real life. I still can't believe that there is anything objectionable about telling it like it is.

The conventions that your husband feels you are flouting seem to have a remarkable staying power. Do you have any ideas why these taboos have lasted for so long?

Our beliefs about childhood are part of our general outlook on life. Americans have a naively optimistic view of the world. We feel that we can do anything providing we buckle down and try hard. We are an unintellectual as well as an antiliterary country. We like leaders who give us simple answers. One of the reasons Freud's theories are still not really accepted in America is that he pointed out that there are darker sides to human life. There are self-destructive urges, not only in the world at large, but also in ordinary people, even in children. And, of course, he stressed the importance of sexuality. These ideas still run against the current of American thought.

Many taboos are related to sexism. Accepting females as sexual beings is still terrifying to many men and even some women. In kids' books sometimes teenage boys are allowed to have a sex life, but almost never girls. The idea that girls, nice, friendly, intelligent girls—the same ones who could be someone's daughter or someone's sister—might masturbate or want to have sex goes against many of our stereotypes. I'm afraid many of these taboos are too deeply rooted to go away very soon, if ever.

Do you think there will come a time when children's literature will no longer be restricted by taboos?

No, I don't. I feel much more pessimistic now than when I published my first children's book, *Mom, the Wolf Man and Me,* in 1972. Back then I thought that these taboos were so preposterous and punitive that they would just gradually vanish. I thought that the success of books like mine would show that kids have a need for honesty and realism in their fiction. Well, the books have succeeded, but mainly because the kids themselves have sought them out and bought them in paperback. Librarians are still nervous about realistic children's novels.

How do you generally respond when your books come under attack?

Of course, at some level I'm hurt, as all people are by rejection of what they perceive as a misunderstanding of what they are trying to say. I've seen some authors leave the field or back off, whereas I feel like going full steam ahead. I guess I have a more confrontational personality. Whatever the case, I have made no attempt to water down my children's books, nor will I ever.

At times I try and tell myself that there is something invigorating about being in a field that is embattled. I only wish that it was changing more rapidly. I wish I weren't seeing it go backwards. But I attribute this to the repressive political era we are now going through. When it lifts, things may change again.

What kind of attacks affect you most?

The attacks by the people on the far right don't hurt me much. They can even help me raise important issues. What saddens me is the lack of attention that children's book authors get from the literary establishment. Like authors of adult fiction, we would like people to respond seriously to our books. Yet they are usually just reviewed in a brief paragraph or often ignored altogether. There is very little literary criticism, no matter how loosely one would define that term.

There's also the tendency for children's book critics to devote all of their attention to what one librarian once sardonically referred to as the "N and N's"—Newberys and Notables. She meant the books that win prizes and awards and are largely despised by kids. The more kids like certain books, the more these critics regard them as suspect. The very fact that my books are popular among kids is used as evidence that I'm not literary.

Because kids like books by you and Judy Blume, some of your critics argue that you only write for the market. They are essentially accusing the two of you of being money hungry. How do you respond to this charge?

Every writer wants to make money and be read. Judy and I have paid dearly for sticking to our principles and will continue to do so. Being banned may help you gain readers, but it also denies you access to library markets.

How would you typify your most recent books?

I'm interested in what some call the crossover book. I want to write books that are written in the same way that adult books are written, that is, books that are just as long, just as complex, and that have just as many points of view—but in which the main character is a teenager. Publishers still don't know what to do with these books. They ask, "What is it really? Is it *really* an adult book or is it a children's book?" I answer, "Why does it have to *really* be anything?" But they say it has to be for marketing. *Give and Take,* one of my more recent books, is a perfect example. It's about an eighteen-year-old boy who is a regular donor at a sperm bank. It's a young adult book, but in hardcover it was published as an adult book simply to avoid the mass hysteria of some library journals.

Is it common for publishers to market controversial adolescent books as adult books?

Definitely. I just read *Less Than Zero,* a first novel by a young man named Bret Easton Ellis. It's about a bunch of debauched, extremely wealthy college kids who come home to L.A. They sleep with anything that moves, and they take any drug that they can lay their hands on. What if his characters were in high school at the ages of fifteen or sixteen? They could have obviously been doing similar things at that age. But a book about such kids would have trouble getting into print. Adults don't want to read about high school kids. This extreme hardcore realism is still verboten in the kids' book world.

I look at all of these taboos, and I just want to throw my hands up in consternation and amazement. All they do is make kids turn off to reading even more and wallow in the most idiotic television shows and puerile movies.

Have your publishers ever tried to impose restrictions on your writing?

The first editor to whom I sent *Mom, the Wolf Man and Me* liked it, but wanted the mother to be divorced, not unmarried, and she didn't want her to have a boyfriend who slept over. This went against the statement I was trying to make. I was trying to say that a woman can raise a child alone and that child can have a wonderful childhood. If the mother had been divorced, I wouldn't have been saying quite the same thing. I was also trying to show that mothers do have sex lives whether they are married or not. Well, those ideas were considered radical even then. Luckily I found an editor who said, "Fine, we'll publish it the way it is."

All along, up to the present, publishers have been nervous about my books. I feel I've proved to them that my books do well and have an ardent audience, but they are still worried and frequently ask for changes. For example, in *Angel Face,* one of my more recent books, they didn't want the mother to commit suicide at the end of the book. They saw it as too much of a "downer."

I've had to look hard for the few editors who really believe in what I'm saying. I've always been able to find them, but there are not many. Even editors, whom I see as being more open than many librarians, are frightened.

Almost all your early children's books had girls as the protagonists, but *Beginners' Love, Angel Face, Snapshots,* and some of your other more recent books are about boys. Do you plan to continue to write about boys?

Some publishers have told me to stop writing about boys because they claim boys don't read as much fiction as girls do.

This is probably true. Males of all ages seem to read more nonfiction. But I feel that there must be some boys out there who are tired of rereading *Catcher in the Rye* and don't just want to read about how to fix cars or take apart tanks. I want to write for them.

One thing that annoys me is that they put covers on the paperback editions that make my books told from a boy's point of view look like they are for girls. The hardback covers are better, but the paperback editions look like romance novels. I doubt a boy would be encouraged to pick them up.

It's not that I'll never write about girls again, but right now I want to write about boys, the kind of boys I knew when I was growing up, the kind who in today's world are sometimes termed wimps. I admire boys who are able to resist or question the macho ethic. It takes a lot of courage to look at that whole row of hideous values and say take it away!

Has the increase in censorship activity made it more difficult for children's authors to write about controversial subjects?

Perhaps it has for new authors. I'm very glad I became established at a time when there was more receptivity. My sales may have gone down a little, but my books are still doing well. Because of that, I may take more chances than an author who is just starting out. But I hope new authors will take those chances anyway. I think we have helped pave the way for them.

Have you had any encounters with the people who want to ban your books?

It's very hard to have a meaningful dialog with these people because many of them have no knowledge of literature. I was once on a panel with a woman from some right-wing group, and I happened to mention *Madame Bovary*. She looked puzzled and asked, "Madame who?" I still debate them, though. I like to speak. I always think that there might be some people who see me as a menacing person, and maybe they'll be reassured when they see I'm a somewhat shy middle-aged woman, married over twenty years to the same man, who loves family life. I tell them truthfully that I've never written anything that I wouldn't want my own daughters to read.

What do you feel are the underlying motives of the people who call for the banning of your books?

Fear. One of the fears is that children will do what they read about in books. This fear is based on the false belief that children would never have had the thought without the book. They would never have thought about masturbating, say, but the second they read about it, that's all they'll do. Maybe they'll never practice the piano again! It's the same with sexuality. These people want to believe that their children are living in a little cocoon with no contact with the outside world.

It's also handy to have a scapegoat. They see their own children growing up to reject their values, and they want to blame someone. Often it's their own rigidity which has encouraged their kids to seek other answers. But it's easier for them to blame the books.

I've gotten letters from a few of these people, and some of them claim that my books tell kids that "everything is okay." I'm not saying that. I have my own very vehement and I hope well-thought-out sense of values. But I'm not interested in punishing people. If a character in one of my books has a love affair, she is not going to get killed in the end and she's not always going to get pregnant. Even if I believed in God, it wouldn't be the kind of god who strikes people dead for being human.

Robert Cormier

Robert Cormier is now known primarily as a children's author, but his professional writing career predates the publication of his first children's book by thirty years. He published his first short story in 1944 while he was still a student at Fitchburg State College in Fitchburg, Massachusetts. After graduating, he became a journalist and held various positions at the *Worcester Telegram and Gazette* and the *Fitchburg Sentinel.* He never, however, lost his interest in creative writing. In addition to working on short stories, he wrote several adult novels, three of which were published during the 1960s. In the early 1970s, he began writing a book about teenagers which came out in 1974 under the title *The Chocolate War.* Since then he has written several more young adult novels, including *I Am the Cheese* (1977), *After the First Death* (1979), *The Bumblebee Flies Anyway* (1983), and *Beyond the Chocolate War* (1985).

Cormier's young adult novels have been subjected to numerous censorship attempts, but the reasons his book have been attacked differ somewhat from the reasons Judy Blume's and Norma Klein's books have been censored. His books have been accused of being too critical of authority figures, of presenting an overly pessimistic view of human nature, and of dealing with subject matter that could upset children. Perhaps the most common complaint, however, relates to the way he ends his books. Unlike most of the children's authors who came before him, Cormier does not believe that children's books must have happy and optimistic endings, and it is largely because of his downbeat endings that his books have aroused so much controversy.

Why do so many people feel that all children's books should have happy endings?

I'm not sure where this preoccupation with happy endings comes from. Perhaps it comes from fairy tales since so many of them end with the line, "And they lived happily ever after." But if you look at nursery rhymes, you'll find that many have unhappy endings. In "Rock-a-bye, baby," the cradle comes crashing down. In "Jack and Jill," the kids tumble down the hill and hurt themselves in the process.

I don't think that having a happy ending should be one of the requirements of a children's book. Kids want their books to reflect reality, and they know that the good guys don't always win. They know that the bully doesn't always get his comeuppance in the end. Of course, I certainly don't believe that every children's book should have an unhappy ending, but there should be room for some that do.

When you first plotted out *The Chocolate War*, did it occur to you that the book's ending would be a source of controversy?

Soon after it came out, some reviewers called it a ground-breaking children's book. They seemed to think that I had set out to write an unhappy ending in order to break some taboo. I didn't do that. I was just writing a novel about the adolescent experience, which I was interested in because I had three teenagers in the house at the time. Initially, though, I did not have a young adult audience in mind. When I first started writing the book, I didn't give much thought to who was going to read it. Back then, I certainly didn't think of myself as a children's author.

**At what point did you start to view *The Choco-
late War* as a book for young readers?**

I was about a third into the book when my agent called and
asked me what I was working on. I told her, "I'm writing this
crazy thing about kids selling chocolates in a high school. I
can't imagine who's going to read it, but I'm having fun with
it." She seemed interested and said, "That sounds like a YA." I
honestly had not heard of the term before, and I had to ask her
what she meant. I must have seemed a bit uneasy with the
designation because she told me, "Don't worry about it. Just
write the book and let me worry about the market." And that's
what I did.

Once I was through with it, I put it in her hands, and
she sent it around. Four major publishers refused to publish it.
One rejected it on the grounds that it was neither a kids' book
nor an adult book. The other three liked most of it, but they
wanted me to change the ending. On one occasion, I was
almost tempted to make the change. One publisher offered me
a five-thousand-dollar advance and promised to spend a lot of
money promoting the book, but they insisted that I give the
book a more upbeat ending. Well, five thousand dollars was
very hard to turn down, but I couldn't bring myself to make
the change. I knew if I altered the ending it would jar with the
whole flow of the book. Luckily for me, my agent then sent
the book to Fabio Coen at Pantheon, and he agreed to publish
it without changing my ending.

**Did Fabio Coen express any qualms about the
book when he accepted it?**

He did suggest one change. I had a chapter in the book that
bothered him. It was a pretty graphic chapter, and it had to do

with masturbation. In the chapter, Archie was making plans for the big fight at the end of the book, and he was having trouble deciding how to arrange the whole thing. In his frustration, he started masturbating, and at the moment he climaxed he thought of the idea of the lottery. I was trying to show how sex and power were linked together in Archie's mind. In some ways, though, the chapter seemed out of place, even to me. It wasn't that I felt that masturbation shouldn't be included in a book for young readers. In fact, I mentioned it in passing at several other points in the book. But I wasn't sure if this chapter contributed anything essential to the story. When my fourteen-year-old daughter asked to read the manuscript, I decided to give her the book without the chapter. After she finished it, I asked her if there seemed to be a gap toward the end, and she said, "What do you mean, Dad? I didn't see any gap." Consequently, I wasn't surprised when Fabio Coen criticized the chapter. He thought it was cleverly written but didn't add anything to the story. Although he never insisted that I take it out, he asked me to think about it, and I ended up agreeing with him.

When was the first time that *The Chocolate War* came under attack?

I realized I had written a controversial book soon after it came out. *Booklist* published a review within a month or so after the publication of the book, which really took me to task and accused me of writing an overly cynical book and suggested that I was undermining moral values. So I knew I was in trouble right away, but I never thought it would lead to censorship. However, it was not long after the book came out in paperback that I began hearing about censorship attempts. The first case that I know of occurred in Groton, Massachusetts. A few parents were upset that the book was being taught in a communications class for eighth graders, and they attempted to have it taken off the reading list. They didn't succeed, but warning labels were put on it, and as a result, the book was looked at differently. That's why I say that in censorship cases, even when you win you lose.

After the Groton case, the book continued to come under periodic attacks. Sometime in the early 1980s the attacks became a bit more frequent. In the last two years, however, the number of cases has skyrocketed.

Have any of your other books been censored?

Until 1986, *The Chocolate War* was the only one of my books that attracted censors, but then suddenly *I Am the Cheese* came under attack. For practically ten years it had gone unchallenged. Some people criticized it for being too complex or critical of government, but no one tried to ban it as far as I know. But in 1986 there were at least three attempts to censor it—two in Massachusetts and one in Florida. All three of these attempts succeeded. It makes me wonder whether these censorship efforts are more organized than people think.

In addition to disliking your endings, many of the people who want to ban your books say that you use too many swear words. How do you respond to this charge?

It amazes me when people think that they can obliterate certain words from their children's lives by banning books. If these people ever rode a school bus or walked down a corridor in any junior high school, they'd be in for a shock. The words that upset these people are heard so frequently that it would be impossible for a kid not to be aware of them even if the kid never saw them in a book.

Perhaps the reason these people place so much attention on the language in books is that the words appear in print. It's true that when words appear in print they carry more authority. I discovered that when I worked as a reporter. I wrote some articles that I didn't think were that good, but when they came out in print with headlines on top of them, they seemed more significant. On the other hand, when you are reading a book, it's a private experience. It would seem to me that reading a four-letter word to yourself would be less offensive than hearing it in a public movie theater. And yet these people almost always focus more on books than movies or television. They might complain about television, but it's the books that they burn.

Are there any words that you feel uncomfortable using in your children's books?

When writing dialog, an author's personal taste can easily conflict with the speech patterns of real kids. There is a four-letter word, for example, that I have never put into any of my books. It's an ugly word, and I don't use it in my own speech. It's possible, though, that tomorrow I might find I have a character who wouldn't use any other word, and then I'll use it. So far I have not had to resort to it. Other writers, however, find it effective, and they should have the freedom to use it. I would not impose my personal standards onto other people, and I would hope that they would not impose theirs onto me.

What are the underlying reasons why some parents are so determined to shelter their children from such things as swear words?

Many adults, and certainly most parents, have a natural tendency to protect children, to shelter them from bad things, to make life easier for them. I know as a father I have tried to keep my kids from being hurt or from being exposed to terrible sights, so I can sympathize with the impulse to shelter children. But unfortunately, this impulse often leads parents to attempt to control the entirety of their children's lives. This is not only wrongheaded; it's impossible. Children start thinking on their own while they are still in the sandbox. Parents have to accept the fact that they are not always going to be the sun around which their children orbit. Once you acknowledge these things, you can grow with them, you can develop a real relationship with them. But if you try to control your children's fantasies, thoughts, and emotions, you'll just drive your children away from you.

These parents don't seem to realize that kids live part of their lives outside of the home and the classroom. They are part of the world. They watch television, ride buses, see newspaper headlines, and go to movies. Most kids have heard of corruption or terrorism or sexuality, and I see no reason not to deal with these subjects in children's books.

I should point out, though, that when I'm writing a book, I don't think about these issues. I think more in terms of characters and situations. When I started working on *After the First Death*, for example, I didn't say, "Now I'm going to write a book about terrorism." I was writing about a brave girl on a bus and a young man who was innocent to the point of being a monster. It was only after I finished the book and somebody asked me what it was about that I said, "I suppose it's about terrorism." I try not to put these kind of labels on my books, but once they are in the hands of the critics they start collecting labels.

Some of your critics say that the sort of subjects that you write about could be upsetting to young readers. Do you ever worry about this issue?

I really don't worry about what a fourteen or fifteen-year-old can absorb. If I worried about every scene that might upset some kid somewhere, I'd have to stop writing. As I see it, I owe my readers an honest story that is not exploitative or sensational. But if some kid finds the story upsetting, I'm afraid that's just too bad. I know this sounds harsh, but a writer can't afford to take responsibility for each of his readers.

In your dealings with censors, what is the thing that disturbs you the most about them?

The most frightening thing about censors is their complete sense of righteousness. They remind me of the young terrorist I wrote about in *After the First Death.* Like the terrorist, they are so convinced of the righteousness of their cause that they don't even think about what they are doing to other people. They sincerely think that they are doing the right thing when they try to ban a book. It doesn't seem to occur to them that other people might not feel the same way about the book.

Something else that disturbs me is the way they treat their children. I can't help but feel sorry for these people's kids. I know of a case where *The Chocolate War* was being taught, but one girl in the class wasn't allowed to be in the room when it was being discussed. Her parents insisted that she go to the library and stay there until the discussion ended. She should have had a chance to say, "I don't like this book." She should have been allowed to participate in an open debate. Instead, she was ostracized and made to look strange in the eyes of the other kids. I don't think that's a proper way to treat children.

Does it seem to you that these people are really quite detached from what is going on in their children's lives?

I think so. One of the people who wants to ban *I Am the Cheese* is a good example of this. He dislikes the book because the parents in the story lie to their boy about their family history. This man said that kids reading the book would probably realize that parents lie to their children, and he didn't want his children to think that he was capable of lying to them. To me this is a mind-boggling reason to ban a book. I'm sure his children already realize that he is capable of lying to them. My children certainly know that I might not always tell them the full truth, and I know that they don't always tell me all the truth. This is one of the things that keeps us all living together, and anybody who doesn't recognize that is just fooling themselves.

Does being censored have any benefits?

Just one, and that's that you find yourself in pretty good company. I remember reading a list of books that had recently been banned, and there was *The Chocolate War* in the middle of all these classic books. I felt like sneaking away and hiding. It seemed like too high of praise to have my book listed beside *Romeo and Juliet*.

Some censored children's authors have responded to this problem by leaving the children's book field. Are you ever tempted to do this?

Of course, my first novels were about adults, but since the early 1970s, I've mostly written about adolescents. Well, about a year ago, I decided to write a novel in which the main character was a middle-aged man. I came up with what I thought was a terrific plot and started writing, but I soon became bored with my main character. I was bored with his reactions to things. I was bored with his personality. I realized that for me the adolescent mind is much more interesting to write about. Maybe I'm an arrested adolescent. Whatever the reason, I decided to put the book aside and go back to writing about adolescents. Maybe I'm trapped, but I like it.

As a censored author, do you feel obligated to participate in anticensorship work?

Yes and no. I feel it's important to resist censorship pressures, and I do what I can. I have spoken out against censorship on numerous occasions, and I always lend my support to the people who are defending my books. But, in a way, I resent having to do it. Anything that takes me away from my typewriter or any writer away from their work is, in itself, a victory for the censors. It's another one of those no-win situations.

My biggest frustration in fighting censorship is that the cards are stacked in favor of the censors. There is a man who is trying to ban my books in Florida. He took out a newspaper ad in which he reprinted several lines from *The Chocolate War* and *I Am the Cheese* with the so-called dirty words left blank. And then he said, "If you object to this type of material being taught to your children, write to me." It's hard to counter such an ad. I feel like taking out an ad and saying, "Read the whole book." But it wouldn't work. It's much easier to get people to read nine words with a blank space in the middle than it is to get them to read 75,000 words.

It's the same thing with petitions. What do you say to somebody who rings the doorbell and says, "They're teaching dirty books in the schools. Do you want dirty books taught to your children?" Nobody is going to say, "Yes, I want dirty books taught in the schools." It's easy to appeal to the emotions, and that's where the censors come out ahead. That's why I sometimes feel like I'm fighting fog.

What concerns you the most about the current censorship movement?

I'm most concerned about the forms of censorship that never make the headlines. I recently met a teacher, for example, who wants to teach *The Chocolate War*, but her department head is afraid that the book would cause trouble and won't order it. The book, in other words, wasn't thrown out of the classroom; it was simply prevented from ever entering it. This kind of quiet censorship is going on all of the time.

Then there is the censorship that goes on before books are even published. I know an author whose book wasn't picked up in paperback because of some controversy surrounding it. "From now on," he says, "I'm writing squeaky clean books." It's terrible when authors start to feel they are under this kind of pressure. It's a form of censorship that nobody talks about, but it's happening all too often. I feel that this is the worst kind of censorship because it aborts ideas and stifles the creative act.

Betty Miles

Although Betty Miles usually writes for a somewhat younger audience than does Robert Cormier, she shares his desire to address complex social and political issues in her children's books. Her first novel, *The Real Me,* published in 1974, was one of the earliest children's books to come out of the contemporary feminist movement. Also in 1974, she published a work of nonfiction entitled *Save the Earth! An Ecological Handbook for Kids.* In *All It Takes Is Practice* (1976) and *Sink or Swim* (1987), she deals with the problem of racial prejudice. While not all her novels are focused on particular issues, she never attempts to shelter children from the problems of the real world.

When the censorship of children's books emerged as a problem in the later 1970s, Miles decided to write a children's novel about it. The book, *Maudie and Me and the Dirty Book,* came out in 1980. As the story opens, the central characters, two eleven-year-old girls, begin working as aides in a first grade class. Their job is to select picture books and read them aloud to the class. One of the girls chooses a book that deals with the birth of a puppy. After hearing the story, a first grade boy asks how the puppy got inside the mother dog, and the girl gives him a simple but honest answer. A few parents hear about this incident and demand that the book never be used again. In addition to providing an accurate description of how censorship cases typically develop, Miles does an excellent job of capturing the children's reactions to the whole affair. The book works well both as a novel and as an introduction to the issue of censorship.

When did you first become concerned about censorship?

I began to learn about censorship when I was an associate editor of *The Bank Street Readers* in the 1960s. This was the first national reading series to focus on urban kids and to show black and white children in the illustrations. At that time—a good half dozen years after the Supreme Court decision (*Brown v. Board of Education*) mandating school integration—it was very difficult to sell any publisher the idea of producing an integrated reading series. Dick and Jane and their friends stayed all-white in their fenced-in backyards. Call it censorship, or racism, or publishing conservatism, the result was the same: All American children were learning to read from primers relevant only to some of them. I remember a series of expensive lunches at which one publisher after another explained why it was financially impossible to publish textbooks with black kids in them. Finally, Macmillan took the step, but cautiously; along with *The Bank Street Readers,* they continued to publish and market their all-white reading series.

Soon after this, I was faced with another issue that introduced me to the complexities of First Amendment rights. The state of Texas was considering adoption of *The Bank Street Readers.* Without state adoption no school district could purchase them, but at the time no textbook could *be* adopted unless all those associated with the books signed a pledge saying they were not Communists. I got a routine form from Macmillan asking me to sign the pledge. I was outraged; I wasn't a Communist, but I didn't think my political beliefs were anyone else's business. In the end, with a letter of protest, I signed, feeling my personal discomfort with the pledge was less important than getting the series adopted in Texas so that kids could use the books. This was my introduction to the hard truth that it isn't easy to be wholly pure in one's moral stands. I hope it's made me a bit more empathetic with other people's dilemmas.

What kinds of attacks have your books been subjected to?

First, let's acknowledge that there's a real difference between ordinary complaints and censorship attempts. Authors get complaints all the time. Some are rather amusing. I once wrote a picture book called *The Cooking Book* in which I explained how young children could prepare simple things like sandwiches. Well, somebody wrote to my editor and said, "I won't buy the book for my library because it didn't tell children to wash their hands first." I certainly don't call that censorship— it was just a letter from a person who thought she knew better than me. And, in fact, it's a good idea for anyone to wash up before cooking.

The trouble is that even minor complaints make publishers nervous—especially the reprint publishers who run the school book clubs. And sometimes they overreact, anticipating problems before they occur. Several years ago, a book club editor conducted a routine search through my book *All It Takes Is Practice,* which she had agreed to reprint, looking for words or sentences that might, as she put it, "be red flags to parents." Not surprisingly, she found some that worried *her*— even though not a single complaint had been made about them to the publisher of the hardcover edition. She asked me to delete a two-sentence passage in which a kid remarks that she sees nothing wrong with an interracial couple getting married, "if they love each other." I protested. The editor agreed to discuss the issue with her editorial board—and the board responded by saying the whole *book* should not be published! I call *that* censorship.

What else would a book club editor view as "a red flag"?

Some of the things that book club editors regularly want to delete are four-letter words and what they consider to be sexually related words. I've allowed some of these deletions but only under the condition that they don't affect the tone of my characters' voices. What really bothers me is being asked to substitute words that my characters would never use. Once, for example, an editor asked me to change the word "sexy" in reference to a nightgown a twelve-year-old had brought to a pajama party to "snazzy." That's not the sort of word my character would ever think of saying, and I refused to allow the change. I lost, I should add, a large book club sale by refusing. *That's* censorship.

Why are book clubs so cautious about what they publish?

Book clubs sell their books directly through the schools. Kids bring home a list or a catalog, choose the books they want, and ask their parents to buy the books. Book clubs worry that parents will be more critical about books they've paid for themselves, and that the school system has at least implicitly condoned, than about books that are simply available in a library. It's easy to understand why book club editors feel under a lot of pressure—and today, realistically, they *are* under pressure from highly organized would-be censors. But I still think that editors sometimes give in before there is any need to give in. They anticipate problems that may not even exist, or yield before the fact to complaints that *might* be made, by a very small number of critics. I wish that those critics, who seem to feel authors are out to corrupt their children, could read the letters many of us get from grateful kids who have found our books comforting and encouraging.

Have you seen any changes in the types of things that provoke would-be censors?

Lately the censors are objecting to much more than what they call "foul language"—now they are beginning to question the morality of whole books. This trend was brought home to me when my first novel, *The Real Me*, published in 1974, was recently attacked by a New Jersey parent. Until now, the only complaints I had received were about the father saying "damn it." But this parent found much more wrong with the book. According to the lengthy form that she filled out, my book "teaches negative values," "challenges existing mores," "fosters liberation from absolute standards of moral conduct," and has "a powerful image (sometimes negative) on children's view of the world." All that in a short, sometimes funny book about a young girl learning to speak up for her rights—one that was judged a "Book of the Year" by the Child Study Association.

Some people argue that the selection process that librarians and teachers use can function as a subtle form of censorship. What are your thoughts on this issue?

Of course selection can be censorship, but I think we should assume the intelligence, goodwill, and professionalism of librarians rather than trying to second-guess their every decision. Who of us would want the responsibility of book selection if it meant defending every decision to buy, or to discard, a book? Still, I wish all librarians would appreciate the special opportunity they have to widen children's horizons through books. An example: I recently went to my local library, in suburban New York, to look for a book called *Yellow Bird and Me,* by Joyce Hansen. It wasn't on the shelves, so I asked the librarian if she had ordered it. I mentioned that it had received some very good reviews. "Yes, I remember them," she said, looking the title up in one of the review journals. "But there was something . . . oh, yes." She pointed to the words "black teenagers." "If I ordered this," she explained, "it would just sit on the shelf." What she meant was the white kids in this suburban community wouldn't want to read about black city kids.

Is this censorship, or inertia? Whatever you call it, it troubles me.

When did you start writing *Maudie and Me and the Dirty Book?*

I began to write *Maudie* in 1978, but had been thinking about it for a while. A year or so before I started writing I began collecting information on censorship. That's how I work. I have files on many topics; one, for example, is on teenage pregnancy. I've kept up that file for ten years, and while I may never write a book about it, it's important to me to keep the information current, in case I should need it.

Did the censorship attempt that you describe in *Maudie* really occur?

The kinds of censorship attempts described in *Maudie* have happened somewhere in this country—and so have the positive responses—but the book isn't based on any one specific censorship case. The picture book that sparks the controversy in the story really exists, but only in manuscript, in my file drawer. I needed a real story to describe and quote from so I wrote one about a puppy getting born. (I later tried to sell it to my editor, but without luck!)

I gave some thought to using an actual book that had been censored, like *Forever,* but I decided against it. I wanted to write about a case involving a book for younger children— one that I would have absolutely no qualms about reading to a first grader.

Do you have any qualms about *Forever?*

No. Of course, it's not the book *I* would have written—which is another way of saying that I wasn't creative enough, or nervy enough, to make the attempt. Until Judy Blume wrote *Forever,* there simply were no books for teenagers that dealt with the sexual aspect of their relationships. Judy Blume stuck her neck out and did it, and I think all writers—and readers— should be grateful to her, and to her publisher, for leading the way to more openness in adolescent fiction. Criticisms like "most girls wouldn't react that way," or "that's not how I experienced it" miss the point. No single book can reflect every variety of experience. The important thing about *Forever* is that its publication made it easier for all children's books to speak more frankly about sex, and so to portray adolescent life more honestly.

What sorts of things do you think fuel the censors' sense of anger?

Although it is seldom discussed, I think there is an element of class conflict in some censorship cases. Many of the people who want to ban books feel intimidated by everything that books seem to stand for: education, culture, a rich life. They may feel uneasy around people who seem to know so much about books. They feel—often with justification—put down and belittled. Misguidedly or not, many would-be censors are trying to do what they think is right for their kids, and when they find themselves dismissed as a bunch of fools, it's naturally painful to them. There's very little that's more painful than being laughed at. I've been at meetings where supposedly open-minded people snickered at their opponents' mispronunciation of words. If that's how book-reading "intellectuals" behave, I'm not surprised at anti-intellectual rage.

How does this distrust of intellectuals affect some parents' attitudes toward education?

We always talk about the American dream of upward mobility, but I think there has always been a corresponding fear of it. Of course all parents want their children to do well in school, get a good job, be successful—but it's natural for some to worry about what will happen when these children make their way up in the world. Will they still be proud of their parents? Or will they reject them? Parents want their kids to be educated, but not so educated that they grow away. Such parents may come to view books and learning as a threat.

As you know, not all censors are conservative. There are some feminists, for example, who believe in censoring sexist children's books. How do you respond to these people?

I don't agree with them, but that doesn't mean that I'm indifferent to the concerns that they raise. I hate books that demean girls and women. But instead of trying to censor books we don't agree with, I think it's more important to support good, nonsexist books. In the early 1970s, I worked with a group of women in publishing called Feminists on Children's Media.

We produced an annotated reading list of quality, nonsexist children's books called *Little Miss Muffet Fights Back*. I think our work had a really positive effect on editors, publishers, authors, librarians, parents—and, ultimately, on young readers.

How do you respond to the argument that children should not be allowed to read a book until they are mature enough to understand everything the book covers?

I think it's a weak argument. Kids often get more out of a book that challenges them than they do out of one that only covers familiar territory. They might come across something that they are not ready for, but it has been my experience that this isn't a serious problem. I think we all self-censor when we read. For example, sometimes I find I'm unable to read detailed newspaper articles on the torture of political prisoners, and I stop reading. Children do something similar when they come across things that bother them. Either they put the book down or they skip over certain parts. And, of course, kids don't deliberately go out and choose books they think will upset them.

As an author who often addresses social issues in your books, how do you feel when your books are referred to as problem novels?

It really surprised me when I first heard myself described as an author of problem novels. I had thought I was writing about real life—in which, naturally, there are problems! "Problem novel" has become a pejorative term—I've never heard a book described as so-and-so's wonderful problem novel. Unfortunately, implicit in the phrase is the idea that children's books should not address social problems. I disagree. Children, like all the rest of us, are aware of social issues, and care passionately about equality and justice. I think their books should acknowledge, and encourage, such passion.

What do you say to the critics who argue that authors like you are simply trying to cash in on popular topics?

After the publication of *The Real Me,* some reviewers accused me of writing about feminism because it was an "in" topic. In fact, that book grew out of many years of personal experience with sexism. I put a lot of strong feelings and beliefs into that book; to have it dismissed as a quick attempt to capitalize on a popular trend really upset me.

Some critics seem to believe that a cabal of children's book authors gets together to choose trendy topics: "This year let's make it incest . . . " In reality, we are all dismayed to find that someone else has published a book on the same topic we have been working on for a long time. There are bound to be trends in subject matter, because authors listen to what's going on in the world and care about the issues of the day. It's natural to write about the things you care about. I believe authors have the right—and the responsibility—to address social issues. When critics try to undermine this right, they play into the hands of the censors.

Harry Mazer

Before Harry Mazer began writing books for young people in the early 1970s, he had worked as a writer of magazine fiction, a welder, and a sheet metal worker. Mazer's familiarity with life in the blue-collar world can be seen in his books, most of which are about the children of working-class parents. He published his first book, *Guy Lenny,* in 1971 and has since gone on to publish many more, including *Snow Bound* (1973), *The Dollar Man* (1974), *The War on Villa Street* (1978), *The Last Mission* (1979), *The Island Keeper* (1981), *I Love You, Stupid!* (1981), *Hey, Kid! Does She Love Me?* (1984), *When the Phone Rang* (1985), and *The Girl of His Dreams* (1987).

Three of Mazer's books have been targeted by censors: *The War on Villa Street, The Last Mission,* and *I Love You, Stupid!.* In *The War on Villa Street,* Mazer focuses on the tensions between a withdrawn boy and his alcoholic father. Much of the story is set on the streets of a large city, and the dialog generally follows the patterns of street language. Mazer's use of this type of language is the main reason the book has been censored. *The Last Mission,* a novel about a teenager's experiences in the Air Force during World War II, has also been attacked for its realistic dialog. In the case of *I Love You, Stupid!,* Mazer's first novel about a teenage love affair, the issue of language has not played a major role in the attempts to censor the book. Instead, the book has been attacked for dealing with a teenage boy's sexual thoughts and desires.

When you began writing children's books, did you feel any pressure to uphold certain taboos?

Not at all. I entered the field around 1970 at the suggestion of my agent. At the time, I knew very little about what sort of children's books were being published, so my agent gave me two books to read: *Queenie Peavy* by Robert Burch and *Harriet the Spy* by Louise Fitzhugh. Queenie's father was in prison and Harriet was looking at the adult world critically. There were new attitudes here, new subjects, new currents seeping into the quiet, protected waters of children's books. My agent urged me to bring the real world to children's books. I liked the idea and that's what I did.

My first book, *Guy Lenny*, was about a working-class boy who has to choose between his divided parents. I felt no censorship, no taboos, no cautions urged on me by my editor, no warnings that I might be straying or straining the limits. From the first my editors encouraged me to write my books as freely and fully as I could. There was no talk about breaking taboos until the late 1970s.

What sort of things did they start asking you to change?

There had been a little stir of criticism directed at *The Dollar Man,* my third book. The boy in the shower, the suggestion of masturbation. My editor mentioned it to me, not as criticism, or even as a warning, but as something he felt I should know. When I was working on *The Last Mission,* my sixth book, my editor expressed concern about some of the language, the swearing and profanity. Was there, perhaps, more than the field could handle? I sympathized with his concerns, but I didn't see how I could write a realistic novel about war and not use the language of war.

But I did go over the book again and I made changes. The language was more restrained afterward. I thought it caused me to be a little more disciplined and inventive which can only be good. For example, I had the hero comment on how everyone swore in the army and how he felt uncomfortable with it. It seemed like a legitimate compromise considering my audience, but it was a compromise. In the end, the book still came under attack.

Was *The Last Mission* the first of your books to be targeted by censors?

No. My first real bout with the censors was over *The War on Villa Street.* This book is about a boy, Willis Pierce, and his alcoholic father; it's also about a friendship that develops between Willis and a retarded boy. In 1981, two mothers from a small community near Rochester, New York, led a campaign to ban *Villa Street* from their local junior high school library. In their complaint they found, perhaps, thirty words that they felt didn't belong in a book for young people. "Retard" was one of these words.

A committee of teachers and other professionals found the book worthy and said the book had a legitimate place in the junior high. Unfortunately, the school superintendent thought otherwise, and the book, so far as I know, is still off that school's shelves.

Why do would-be censors focus so much attention on the issue of language?

I think their complaints about language often mask other objections and objectives. Language is the censor's foot in the door. It's the way to gag and control the author. What the censors would really like to do is stand behind the author and say, "These are the things you can write and these are the things you can't write." The censors have certain ideas about what children should read. They want exemplary books that teach proper behavior. They want books with happy endings and neat little moral homilies. They want models of goodness, children who don't use "bad" words or talk up to their elders, or God forbid, even think about sex. They want children fenced out of the real world. Never mind the ignorance in the world and young people's need to know. They want children's books to present a safe, predictable, sugarcoated world, a world that never was and never will be. Language is a useful weapon in this campaign. How better to intimidate an author than by denying him his own words.

Have these battles over language affected the way you write?

I'd like to believe that the censors have had no effect on my writing. I think that I resist; I do resist; I don't give ground; I write my books exactly the way I've always written them, aware that I'm writing for young people, but also aware that there is a reality out there that I want reflected in my work.

But, in saying all that, I must add that I write today with an awareness and, yes, a caution that wasn't there when I began writing. I've become "inventive" in my use of language, finding other ways of saying what may be challenged.

The pressure, I say, is heavy on the author and not to be aware of it can be costly. If you're going to resist, you better be aware that the enemy has a foothold in your mind. After all, I earn my living this way and the censors have put a hole in my pocket.

Take book club sales. The book clubs are notoriously

cautious about anything controversial, particularly language or sex. Of my first six books only one sold to the book clubs. When I wrote *The Island Keeper,* I deliberately set out to write a book that the book clubs would accept. I even told myself that this would improve the book because it would make me work harder.

The Island Keeper is about a girl alone on an island. In an early writing of the book, I had a boy on the island unaware that the girl was there watching him. Then, in a subsequent revision, I wrote the boy out—rubbed him out, if you will—because I was afraid his presence might lead to romance and sex. I succeeded in writing a noncontroversial book that was accepted by a book club, but I felt afterwards that I had compromised myself and I regretted it.

Is the language issue the only reason your books have been censored?

Sex, sexuality is another reason. My book *I Love You, Stupid!* has been attacked as pornographic, which is practically laughable. Pornography to me is work that's produced to titillate sexually, to use, vilify, and exploit females for male pleasure. *I Love You, Stupid!* is about the relationship of a boy and a girl, both of them interested in sex. It's about feelings, desires, and anxieties. It's about the sex fantasies of a teenage boy. I'm afraid, however, that in our repressed culture, even acknowledging the existence of sexual thoughts is considered dangerous.

Sex, sex thoughts, our sexuality is not where the danger lies. Sex is life, and the real danger lies in not acknowledging the centrality of our sexuality. Literature, at its best, should bring readers to themselves. When I was a boy, I read to find out about myself, to read about characters like myself who were feeling some of the same things that I was feeling. Not the bravado public stuff, but the true secret, mixed and confused feelings that make us feel like monsters and freaks. That's why I wrote *I Love You, Stupid!;* so boys who read it could say, "That's the way I feel, I'm not the only one, I'm not a freak. . . ."

A controlled literature, a censored literature, which children's books have traditionally been, which teaches morality and behavior, tends to separate readers from their own lives, which is just the opposite of what literature should do.

Why are there so few young adult books that tell about teenage love affairs from the boy's point of view?

Boys don't read love stories. The wisdom says that teenage boys either don't read at all or only read adventure stories, sports, war stories, and fantasy and science fiction. Girls read love stories. That's why the stories are mainly told from a female viewpoint.

It's absurd to think that boys who are profoundly interested in girls and in love are not interested in stories about love. But let's not call them love stories. Call them relationship stories; call them stories of conflict; call them contemporary stories. Just call them stories. That's what I've been writing starting with *I Love You, Stupid!, Hey, Kid! Does She Love Me?,* and *The Girl of His Dreams.* Each of these books is written from the boy's point of view. I write about relationships, about love and sex and the whole fascinating frustrating dance and tug of war that goes on between maturing boys and girls.

Are boys reading these books? I hope so. I know girls read them. But I feel vindicated in writing these books when I get a single letter from a boy who wrote about *I Love You,*

Stupid!, "Marcus is just like me. Now I don't feel so alone anymore."

Of all of the things that would-be censors have said about your books, which one bothers you the most?

The most unfair accusation is that my books drive a wedge between parents and their children. Not my books; the censors themselves drive the wedge. Each time they ignore their kids' questions and concerns and demand behavior to an arbitrary and unrealistic standard they drive the wedge even deeper.

If these parents want to get closer to their kids, they should try to remember what it was like to be a kid themselves. They should try to empathize with their kids' feelings of loneliness and confusion. Instead of censoring their kids' books, maybe they should read them and then talk with their kids about them. If they did this, I think they'd discover that books are bridges, not wedges. Books help us make connections with each other while censorship serves only to drive us apart.

Nat Hentoff

Nat Hentoff first gained public recognition as an authority on jazz musicians and their music, and most of his publications from the fifties and early sixties relate to this subject. In the mid-sixties, though, his interests began to diversify. He began to write about First Amendment issues and soon became known as one of the nation's leading civil libertarians. He also began publishing books for children. His first children's novel, *Jazz Country*, appeared in 1965 and was followed by *I'm Really Dragged but Nothing Gets Me Down* (1968), *Country of Ourselves* (1971), *This School Is Driving Me Crazy* (1976), and *Does This School Have Capital Punishment?* (1981).

Two of Hentoff's books for young adults deal with censorship. *The First Freedom: The Tumultuous History of Free Speech in America* (1980) is a work of nonfiction aimed at high school and college students. In keeping with his intended audience, Hentoff begins the book, not with a historical analysis of the Bill of Rights, but with a lively discussion of the First Amendment rights of students. *The Day They Came to Arrest the Book* (1982) functions as both a novel and a primer on the First Amendment. The story revolves around an attempt to remove *Huckleberry Finn* from a high school reading list on the grounds that the book is racist. Hentoff devotes much of the book to detailing the arguments put forth by the various characters. Although it has been criticized for having a slow plot, the book provides its readers with a solid introduction to the political and philosophical underpinnings of the current censorship debate.

As you make clear in *The Day They Came to Arrest the Book*, there are a wide variety of people who feel that children's reading materials should be censored. Are there any generalizations that hold true for all of them?

For the most part, these people think that they have both a right and a moral duty to control what their children read and think about, and it's not just people on the right who feel this way. Since the election of Reagan, however, the religious fundamentalists have become the most vocal proponents of this view. They feel that his election somehow validated their beliefs about child rearing. Before Reagan, though, there were liberals who tried to ban books from school libraries because of the sexism or racism in the books as they saw it. Those who want to censor, whether they are on the left or the right, feel that there is only one correct way that children should be taught about the world, their country, and themselves.

In what ways do conservative censors differ from liberal censors?

Many conservative fundamentalists feel that it is their responsibility to guide and control nearly every aspect of their children's lives. They're concerned not only about what their kids read, but also about what they are taught in school, the types of friends they play with, the shows they see on television, etc. These parents feel that their children should never be exposed to values that are antithetical to those taught in the home and the church. Such conflict, they feel, would set their kids off on the wrong track, would make it impossible for kids to tell the difference between right and wrong, would even cause kids to feel skeptical about God. In other words, these parents believe it is their job to shape their children's lives, and censoring reading materials is just one part of that job.

Most parents on the left take a considerably more permissive attitude. They don't intervene as much in their children's lives, but they, too, feel it is their responsibility to inculcate their values. Even the most progressive parents try to shape their children's lives. Very few parents that I know of really believe that children should be allowed to come to their own values and judgments. I know leftist parents who would be extremely upset if their child decided to become a corporate lawyer. Still, on the whole, I'd say that leftist parents are less inclined to censor their children's reading.

How do you explain this difference? What is it about fundamentalist parents that predisposes them to become censors?

There are two reasons for this. They may well have a stronger belief in the power of the word. They truly feel that words have the power to transform a child, to turn a child inside out. At the same time, they do not have as much confidence in the child's ability to make sound decisions. Part of this might be tied to their idea that decisions should be based on doctrine rather than on reason.

Some fundamentalists argue that children should not be allowed to make their own decisions because their minds are not yet ready for such responsibility. How do you respond to this?

Being ready is a process. Kids need to learn how to think, not just what to think. The process of thinking is something that kids should be encouraged to engage in throughout their childhood, but especially during adolescence. If you wait until after high school, you've lost valuable time. Kids who've gone through their secondary school life without ever hearing more than one point of view can become intellectually crippled. They can lose their potential for original and independent thought. They can lose their ability to engage in free inquiry.

What do the censors hope to accomplish by preventing their children from reading books that conflict with their own beliefs?

These parents think that by protecting their children they are making their children more resistant, but actually they are making their children more vulnerable. This point was made by Dr. Kenneth Clark, a distinguished psychologist, during one of the times that *Huckleberry Finn* was under attack by a group of black parents. Kenneth, who is black, argued that when you prevent black kids from reading this book because it contains the word "nigger," you are telling them that words are so powerful that you can't do anything about them except hide them or run away from them. He said that's not the way to deal with racism. The way to deal with it is to learn about it and explore its motivations, not run away from it.

When you were raising your own children, did you ever shelter them from beliefs that differ from your own?

We had four kids, all of whom are grown-ups now, and my wife and I made no attempt to feed them just one line. Since my wife is more conservative than I am, we would often have political and moral arguments at the dinner table. Our kids would frequently join these arguments, and they wouldn't always take my side. I think it was a good experience for them. When the time came for them to go forth into the world, they were able to think for themselves because they were used to dealing with a barrage of competing ideas.

Some procensorship parents argue that they are simply trying to improve the quality of their children's education. Is there any validity to this argument?

While I agree that parents should become involved in their children's education, the pressures that these people are putting on our school systems are doing anything but improving public education. Because of these people, teachers are becoming more and more reluctant to encourage children to question and analyze. The Socratic method, which teachers have been using for centuries, is now being avoided because it might offend some parents.

Curricular materials are also being affected. Since most textbook publishers want to avoid censorship battles, they are publishing books that are designed not to offend anyone. That's why you see history books that don't mention religion or science books that hardly deal with evolution. You can't have stimulating books if you aim at the absolute lowest common denominator.

What's so dismaying is that the people who are causing the deterioration of the public schools are sincere when they say that they are trying to improve teaching. They just have a crazy idea of what good teaching is all about. They want the public schools to be run like some of the Christian schools where the kids learn everything by rote memorization. The kids in these schools look like a bunch of automatons, repeating what they are told. That's not education; that's mind control.

In addition to attacking materials used in the classroom, censors often attempt to remove books from libraries. It seems, though, that they have much more success in school libraries than in public libraries. Why is this?

Censorship occurs more frequently in school libraries, in part, because they are under the control of school board members and principals, not librarians. Public libraries, however, are run by librarians, and most public librarians try to follow the American Library Association's "Library Bill of Rights." This document states that so long as a child has a library card he or she can check out any book that circulates in the library, even if the book is in the adult section. If parents don't approve of the books that their children select, then they need to make sure that they are always in the library when their kids are there.

Sometimes librarians place controversial children's books in the adult section of the library. Do you consider this censorship?

Symbolically, it's a form of censorship, and it does make it less likely that a child will just stumble across the book. But if the child is free to move around the library, relocating the book from the children's section to the adult section is not a significant impediment.

I am not aware of any libraries that still restrict children to certain sections of the library, but when I was young, most libraries had rules about which sections kids could and could not use. The library that I used never enforced these rules, but a lot of them did. I had friends who were prevented from checking out a book because it was kept in the adult section.

**Have any of your children's books been cen-
sored?**

I've heard about several censorship attempts involving my
books, but the case I'm most familiar with occurred in a small
junior high school in Alabama. Apparently, *This School Is Driving Me Crazy* was being used with boys who were reluctant
readers. Some of their parents, however, complained about it,
and it was removed from the school. When I heard about this,
I called up the principal and asked why. He said that the
parents objected to the use of the words "damn" and "hell,"
and they also didn't like it when one of the boys in the book
calls another boy "a limp dick." I asked if the book had gone
through any kind of review procedure after the complaint was
made. He said that the school did have a review committee,
and the committee had recommended that the book be kept,
but he decided to overrule the committee because he didn't
want any trouble.

**How should authors respond when their books
are censored?**

I think it helps if the author makes contact with the censors.
Quite often these people deal in abstractions, but the issue
becomes less abstract when a real person calls them up on the
phone and asks, "What's going on with my book? What's the
rationale for trying to ban it?" It might not change their minds,
but at least it forces them to confront the reality of what they
are doing.

**Do you have any advice for people who are con-
cerned about censorship?**

The first thing I recommend that people do is join People for the American Way. This organization is doing a marvelous job of making people aware of the problem of censorship. Also worth joining is the local affiliate of the American Civil Liberties Union. I also think that anticensorship people should organize into local groups or networks and make their presence known at textbook commission hearings, school board meetings, and other places where censors are likely to strike. An effort should be made to monitor censorship efforts and respond to them before they become major cases.

Roald Dahl

In recent years, most of the controversies in children's literature have focused on the authors of realistic books. An important exception to this trend is Roald Dahl, an English author whose children's books are immensely popular in both England and the United States. Although Dahl's first children's book, *The Gremlins,* came out in 1943, it was not until the publication of *James and the Giant Peach* in 1961 that he became a well-known children's author. Since then he has published many fantasy books for children, including *Charlie and the Chocolate Factory* (1964), *The Magic Finger* (1966), *Charlie and the Great Glass Elevator* (1972), *The BFG* (1982), and *The Witches* (1983).

Although much loved by children, Dahl's books have often met with adult disapproval. A number of his books have been accused of being vulgar, excessively violent, and disrespectful toward authority figures. Of all his books, *Charlie and the Chocolate Factory* and *The Witches* are the most controversial. Throughout the late sixties and early seventies, *Charlie* came under frequent attack for being racist. In a widely read article published in the *Horn Book Magazine,* Eleanor Cameron, a prominent literary critic and children's author, went so far as to call *Charlie* "one of the most tasteless books ever written for children." *The Witches,* a story about a confrontation between a young boy and a coven of witches, has attracted the ire of some feminists. Claiming that the book is misogynist, these feminists have successfully led a campaign to ban the book from several libraries in England. This demonstrates that censorship is a problem in England as well as in America and that censorship pressures can come from the political left as well as from the right.

How did you feel when *Charlie and the Chocolate Factory* came under attack?

It was the first time one of my books came under attack, so I naturally felt surprised. In retrospect, though, I don't think it was an unreasonable attack. In writing the book, I had unwittingly portrayed blacks unfavorably. I created a group of little fantasy creatures called Oompa-Loompas, and I said they were pygmies from Africa. I saw them as charming creatures, whereas the white kids in the book were, with the exception of Charlie, most unpleasant. It didn't occur to me that my depiction of the Oompa-Loompas was racist, but it did occur to the NAACP and others. They pointed out that all of the workers were black. Although I don't know of any attempts to censor the book, there was quite an uproar. After listening to the criticisms, I found myself sympathizing with them, which is why I revised the book. Instead of portraying the Oompa-Loompas as black pygmies from Africa, I made them pink and said they were from a remote island.

Have any of your other books caused an uproar?

Of my more recent books, the one that has been attacked most frequently is *The Witches.* It has been banned from school libraries in several cities in England because some feminists claim that it presents women in a bad light. They base their claim on a quote from the beginning of the book in which I say, "A witch is always a woman." They, of course, ignore the next line that says, "A ghoul is always a male." They also ignore the lovely grandmother, who is one of the major characters in the story.

I don't see this as a reasonable attack. It's fine with me if people criticize my books, but it's quite another thing if they ban them.

Have there been any attempts to censor *The Witches* in the United States?

I don't know of any censorship attempts, but I did receive a number of letters from witches who objected to the book. Apparently, there are two or three societies of witches in America, and some of these witches didn't like the way I treated them in the book. One of them said, "This book must be taken off the shelves at once. We are not such bad people." I didn't know how to respond, so I just ignored their letters.

In America the majority of censorship attempts come from the political right. Is this also true in England?

It seems to me that in England more censorship pressures are coming from the left than the right. We have a number of cities that are run by left-wing groups, and these people often try to take certain books out of the schools. Of course, right-wing people have been equally intolerant. It's usually the extremes on either side that want to ban books. Luckily, these people don't speak for the majority. When a national newspaper ran a story about the banning of *The Witches,* letters flooded in from parents and children ridiculing the censors.

Many people feel that children's books should serve some higher purpose, such as teaching moral lessons to children. What do you see as the purpose of your children's books?

My only purpose in writing books for children is to encourage them to develop a love of books. I'm not trying to indoctrinate them in any way. I'm trying to entertain them. If I can get a young person into the habit of reading and thinking that books are fun, then, with a bit of luck, that habit will continue through life. The person who is what I call a fit reader has a terrific advantage over people who are not readers. Life becomes richer if you have the whole world of books around you, and I'll go to practically any length to bring this world to children.

Why are many adults made uncomfortable by your children's books?

I think they may be unsettled because they are not quite as aware as I am that children are different from adults. Children are much more vulgar than grown-ups. They have a coarser sense of humor. They are basically more cruel. So often, though, adults judge a children's book by their own standards rather than by the child's standards.

This is also why it is so difficult to write a book that children like. By the time you are an adult and are able to write well, it's hard to see the world from the child's point of view. There have been a lot of very famous writers who have tried their hand at writing for children but have failed to create enduring books.

Some people say that the adults in your books come across too negatively. How do you respond to this charge?

I generally write for children between the ages of seven and nine. At these ages, children are only semicivilized. They are in the process of becoming civilized, and the people who are doing the civilizing are the adults around them, specifically their parents and their teachers. Because of this, children are inclined, at least subconsciously, to regard grown-ups as the enemy. I see this as natural, and I often work it into my children's books. That's why the grown-ups in my books are sometimes silly or grotesque. I like to poke fun at grown-ups, especially the pretentious ones and the grouchy ones.

Another complaint that one sometimes hears about your books is that they are too violent. What are your thoughts on the inclusion of violence in children's books?

I do include some violence in my books, but I always undercut it with humor. It's never straight violence, and it's never meant to horrify. I include it because it makes children laugh.

Children know that the violence in my stories is only make-believe. It's much like the violence in the old fairy tales, especially the Grimms' tales. These tales are pretty rough, but the violence is confined to a magical time and place. When violence is tied to fantasy and humor, children find it more amusing than threatening.

You are one of the few children's authors to write about bodily functions. Why do you sometimes refer to these subjects?

Children regard bodily functions as being both mysterious and funny, and that's why they often joke about these things. Bodily functions also serve to humanize adults. There is nothing that makes a child laugh more than an adult suddenly farting in a room. If it were a queen, it would be even funnier. I try to capture this type of humor in *The BFG*, but instead of calling it farting, I call it whizzpopping. In fact, I devote a whole chapter to the subject. I put it in because it makes me, with my childish mind, laugh, and I know it makes children laugh.

You clearly place a lot of emphasis on humor. Could you say a bit more on the value of humor in children's literature?

The one magic ingredient you can find in virtually all first-rate children's books is humor. There are a few exceptions—*The Secret Garden,* for example. But most good children's books make children laugh. I am trying to follow in this tradition. If children find my books amusing, if they laugh while they're reading them, I feel I have succeeded. If I offend some grown-ups in the process, so be it. It's a price I'm willing to pay.

Daniel Keyes

Although Daniel Keyes does not call himself a children's author, his first novel, *Flowers for Algernon* (1966), is widely taught in the schools. Recognized by the Science Fiction Writers of America as the best science fiction novel of the year, *Flowers for Algernon* describes the experiences of a mentally retarded man named Charlie who, as the result of a scientific experiment, is temporarily transformed into a genius. Since the book's publication, Keyes has written two more novels: *The Touch* (1968) and *The Fifth Sally* (1980). He has also published *The Minds of Billy Milligan* (1981) and *Unveiling Claudia* (1986), both of which are works of nonfiction.

Since the early eighties, *Flowers for Algernon* has become an occasional target of censors. In 1981 the book was banned from a high school library in Arkansas, and in 1985 it was removed from a ninth grade curriculum in Iowa. In November 1986, a group of parents from Charlotte, North Carolina, launched an attempt to remove the book from a tenth grade reading list on the grounds that the book "contains pornographic material." When asked to back up this claim, a spokesperson pointed to a passage in which Charlie tells a woman, "I want to make love to you." This censorship attempt sparked a community-wide debate during which Keyes visited Charlotte to defend his book. In the end, the school board rejected the attempt to ban the book.

It was during Keyes's visit to Charlotte that this interview was conducted.

How did you react when you first heard that
Flowers for Algernon **was being called pornographic?**

I was absolutely amazed. I'm not even capable of writing graphic sexual scenes. If you read the book carefully, you'll see that there really aren't any sex scenes in the book. When I was writing about Charlie's sexuality, I skirted around the subject. In one scene, Charlie says, "I don't remember what happened." In the other scene, I use symbolic imagery. So I was flabbergasted when I learned that some people were calling the book pornography.

When I thought about it for a while, I realized that they were playing word games. They were afraid to use the word "obscenity" because a book can't be defined as obscene if it has redeeming social, literary, artistic, or political qualities. *Flowers for Algernon* could, therefore, never be considered obscene. So they decided to use the word "pornography" because it's a vague term but one with lots of emotional connotations. Calling the book pornographic was essentially a ploy.

These people often try to create an issue where none exists, and if you react to it in the wrong way, you help to legitimize their absurd claims. This is the problem I grappled with when they called *Flowers for Algernon* pornography. If I start to argue with them, it sounds as if I'm defending the pornographic passages when, in fact, there are no pornographic passages.

On the one hand, you would like to ignore their ridiculous charges and deprive them of the benefit of being taken seriously. But on the other hand, if you don't take a stand against their agenda, it will continue to grow, just as a cancer grows if left unchecked.

Some of the people who tried to ban *Flowers*
for *Algernon* said that it would be all right to give the

book to older children, but it should be kept from children below a certain age. How do you respond to this line of reasoning?

What they are trying to do is draw a line. They're saying, "If a child is twelve or under, he may not read this." But if the schools give them that victory, they will come back in a year or two and say that eleven-year-olds shouldn't be allowed to read it either. It's all part of a broader attempt to test their limits.

Certain individuals who are having mental problems often go through a phase known as testing the limits. They'll push and push just to test their power. I think we are seeing something analogous to this with the censors. They, too, want to see how far they can go and how many people will support them. Well, in Charlotte they went beyond their limits. They got pushed back, but they will try again. They will test with other books since it doesn't cost them anything but a little time.

Have you had any other problems with censorship?

I have had some problems with the short story that *Flowers for Algernon* is based on. There is a textbook publisher who wants to include the story in an anthology, and their editor sent me the version they want to use. When I looked at it, I saw that they had edited out all sorts of things, including the words "saloon," "mazel tov," and "cigarette." I wrote to them and said, "If you want to publish the story without censoring it, let me know and I'll send you the release form." They then wrote back and said that they had checked the other anthologies in which the story had appeared and had found two where the publishers had deleted several swear words. They asked,

"Please allow us, at least, to do what they did." I said that they could as long as they indicated that this was a special edited version. I was very upset, though, because I had never been told by the other publishers that they were going to tamper with my story. All of this suggests to me that there is a movement afoot to bowdlerize the stories in textbooks without the public knowing it and sometimes without the authors knowing it either. It's being done in secret.

It troubles me when editors and publishers say that they are censoring stories, not because they believe that what they are doing is right, but because they are afraid of someone else. They are afraid that some group will ban their textbook from the schools. It would be defensible if the editor said, "I think this word has to go because it's wrong in this context. The character wouldn't say that." That's valid even though I as a writer might fight it. How do you respond, though, to the editor who says, "I believe in what you've written, but it must be changed to please so-and-so"?

When editors start to suppress ideas because they are afraid, it's a clear sign that we are moving in the direction of a more totalitarian society.

How does this type of censorship activity affect the writing process?

It has a chilling effect. You are sitting at your writing desk, and you are about to use a certain word when suddenly your fingers start to tremble. And you ask yourself, "Do I really need to use that word?" This is where the young writer is more likely to be frightened into compromise than the well-established writer, but even the established writers are feeling the pressure.

How would you typify the mind-set of the people who want to ban books?

They have an isolationist mentality. I think this has something to do with why they are afraid of *Flowers for Algernon*, for it's a story about a man's search for compassion and love. These people are suspicious of love. Love is giving. Love is opening your arms. Love is being involved with other people. Today's conservatives are too afraid to love. They are locking themselves up in their homes and trying to isolate themselves from the rest of the world. They are especially trying to keep their children away from anyone who thinks differently from themselves. It comes under the romantic guise of going back to the old ways when we were a frontier society and children stayed on the farm with their parents except when they went to the one-room school. These people say they want to go back to our good old traditions, but what they are really trying to do is turn the clock back.

There is among some of these people a sense of powerlessness. They can't control the way the world works, but they feel that they can still control their children. Banning books is an attempt to say, "I have power over my children. I can put blindfolds on them and plug up their ears. So long as they are under my roof, I have complete control over them." The irony is that children who are brought up in a home of total repression are likely to rebel when they come of age. Rebellion against parents is part of human nature, but the greatest rebellion is against the totalitarian parent. Children from such backgrounds are likely to explode. Young people who are brought up in more open homes, where they are permitted to read and where full discussion is encouraged, are generally better equipped to deal with the real world.

One of the charges that censors are making against many of the books that are taught in the

schools is that the books advocate the religion of secular humanism. What are your thoughts on this matter?

It seems to me that they are trying to create a bogus religion out of two neutral words. What they are really doing is creating a straw man. What we are seeing is a classic technique of propagandists—the technique of attaching a false label to something you don't believe in and then using that label as a weapon. The label becomes a rallying cry, and secular humanism has become a rallying cry for the fundamentalists. The other propagandist technique that they're using is repeating their charge over and over again. They hope that if they say that secular humanism is a religion often enough it will make it so. McCarthy used similar tactics. He attached the label of Communism to anything he disliked. Nowadays the fundamentalists are doing the same thing, only they are using a new label.

How worried are you about the current censorship trend?

I'm afraid of censorship, but I'm still hopeful. I guess I've always been enough of an idealist to believe that ideas will survive. It's very hard to suppress ideas. You can burn a book. You can even imprison its author, but the ideas in the book have a wonderful way of living on.

Maurice Sendak

The publication of Maurice Sendak's *Where the Wild Things Are* in 1963 marked a major turning point in Sendak's career. It not only won him his first Caldecott Medal and all the acclaim that goes along with winning this award, but it also branded him as one of America's most controversial picture book authors. The controversy stemmed from Sendak's portrayal of the inner workings of a child's mind. A number of parents, librarians, and critics criticized Sendak for dealing so directly with this type of material. They argued that children would find the book confusing or frightening. Sendak, however, went on to deal with psychological themes in several of his other picture books, including *Higglety Pigglety Pop! or There Must Be More to Life* (1967), *In the Night Kitchen* (1970), and *Outside Over There* (1981). He has also been involved with opera, ballet, and film productions that focus on psychological issues.

Although *Where the Wild Things Are* has generated a considerable amount of controversy, *In the Night Kitchen* is the book for which he is most frequently attacked. These attacks generally relate to the nude pictures of Mickey, the central character in the story. Sendak was the first major picture book author to break the taboo against nudity, and as a result the book has been the subject of numerous censorship battles. In some cases, the book has been banned from libraries while in others it has been defaced by people who have drawn diapers on Mickey. The book was first censored in the early seventies, and it has remained a favorite target of censors ever since then.

What was your initial reaction to the controversy surrounding *In the Night Kitchen*?

I thought it was absurd when I first heard that some people were banning it and taking Magic Markers to it. I couldn't believe that anyone could find the depiction of a boy's genitals so upsetting. After all, the pictures of Mickey aren't any more graphic than many of the classic paintings of the Christ child.

It is hard to understand these people because their state of mind is so irrational, but my guess is that they are upset by more than Mickey's nudity. I think they also disapprove of Mickey taking pleasure in his body. These people seem to disapprove of nearly all forms of sensuality, even those that aren't directly sexual in nature.

What do they hope to accomplish by banning *In the Night Kitchen*?

They are trying to keep their children in the dark about their own bodies. They seem to think that children are in complete ignorance of their genitals, and they dislike my book because it threatens this ignorance. It's as if my book contains secret information that kids would be better off not knowing. This whole idea, of course, is ridiculous. Kids take an interest in their genitals at a very early age and are generally quite open about expressing this interest. It's only after they are made to feel ashamed of their bodies that they stop being so open. Their interest doesn't disappear: they just learn not to talk about it.

Were there any other reasons why *In the Night Kitchen* was attacked?

Some critics said that *Night Kitchen* is like a comic book, which is true. I loved comic books as a child, and I deliberately borrowed from the comic book form when I was working on the book. This bothered the people who dismiss comic books as vulgar trash. It bothered them that a major figure in children's literature would devote a whole picture book to a popular form that they despised.

Was *Where the Wild Things Are* ever censored?

Not many people tried to censor it, but it was certainly controversial. The attack that did the book the most harm came from Bruno Bettelheim. He condemned it in an article for a women's magazine although at the time he had not even read the book. He simply based his judgment on someone else's summary of it. Because of his article, all sorts of people said that the book was psychologically harmful to children. This hurt the book, and it hurt me. Since then Bettelheim has come full circle, but the damage had already been done. He is a very intelligent man, and I admire his book on fairy tales, but I still feel that his attack on my book was unfair.

Were any of your other books censored?

I once got into trouble over a book called *Some Swell Pup* because I showed a dog defecating. It's a realistic book about how to raise a puppy, and one of the points I make is that you should not get angry when your puppy craps on the floor because its musculature may not be developed enough for it to control itself. I illustrate this point with a picture that includes some little droppings. Well, there were people who cut this page out of the book. I would think that anybody who has raised a dog would know that this is part of real life, but these people seem incapable of dealing with real life.

The film version of *The Nutcracker* that you worked on has aroused some controversy. Can you explain why?

A number of critics accused us of ruining a classic Christmas story when, in fact, our version is much truer to the E. T. A. Hoffmann story than most versions. All we tried to do was bring back some of the passion and psychological overtones that Hoffmann had put into the story. If you read *Nutcracker,* you'll see that it's not about Sugar Plums; it's mostly about a girl's sexual awakening. We simply took Hoffmann at his word, and for this we got our knuckles rapped. The critics were annoyed or, in some cases, enraged with the film. Their anger was much like the anger that my books sometimes spark. In both cases, it reflects a desire to deny the psychological complexity of children.

Several critics say that your work is influenced by psychoanalytic theory. Is this an accurate interpretation?

It's basically accurate. I'm not a complete convert to psychoanalysis, but I think much of it is still valid and valuable. While I don't see Freud as a god, I do think he was a genius. He had great insights into the human mind. I realize, of course, that it is no longer fashionable to be interested in psychoanalysis, but that doesn't matter much to me.

Has the controversy surrounding your work had any impact on your career?

It has affected me. I love to create for a young audience, but I'm tired of the battle over what is and is not appropriate for children. One of the reasons I was initially attracted to ballet and opera is that they offer me more flexibility in terms of subject matter. I could do things on stage that I couldn't do in a picture book.

I find this whole censorship business very worrisome. Some people think that I'm too well established to be hurt by it, but that isn't true. I still think it will all go away, but it's taking much longer than I originally thought. I plan to sit it out, but I worry about the younger people in the field. They need the kind of encouragement that was given to me when I started, and the current climate is anything but encouraging.

John Steptoe

When John Steptoe published *Stevie,* his first picture book, in 1969, he was still a teenager. The book's critical and commercial success quickly established Steptoe as one of the most promising picture book authors to come out of the black community. Steptoe made good on the promise, producing such picture books as *Uptown* (1970), *Train Ride* (1971), *My Special Best Words* (1974), *Daddy Is a Monster . . . Sometimes* (1980), *The Story of Jumping Mouse* (1984), and *Mufaro's Beautiful Daughters* (1987). Most of Steptoe's early books are set in the inner city and focus on the experiences of black children. In some of his more recent books, however, he has incorporated material from other sources, including Native American and African folklore.

Steptoe's most controversial book, *My Special Best Words,* is about the daily experiences of a three-year-old girl and her one-year-old brother, who is just learning how to use the toilet. While toilet training is just one aspect of the book, it is the reason the book came under attack. Steptoe argues, though, that there are more subtle forms of censorship than direct attacks on books. The scarcity of black picture book authors is, according to Steptoe, the result of an indirect form of censorship.

Do you see any relationship between censorship and racism?

I'm afraid so. After doing this type of work for nearly twenty years, I've concluded that the industry is inherently hostile toward blacks. Now people might say, "Hey, John Steptoe, you're being treated nicely. Your books are being published. You've won awards. How can you make such a claim?" And they're partially right. I am being treated nicely, but I'm one of the only blacks who is doing picture books these days. At a lot of the children's literature conventions I attend, I'm the only black author. When you realize how few blacks are in the picture book field, it's hard not to conclude that it isn't an accident. As I see it, this is a form of censorship. It might be indirect censorship, but it's just as effective as book banning.

Have you discussed this issue with the publishers of picture books?

When you try to talk with them about it, they usually squirm and make excuses. There are exceptions, of course, but most of them will say, "We would like to publish more books by blacks, but it's company policy to only publish established authors." Or, "We would like to, but we have not seen any good manuscripts lately." Or, "We would like to, but books about blacks don't sell very well anymore." These problems may well be true, but there is more than one way to react to them. You can choose to hide behind them, or you can work to solve them.

Was there ever a time when publishers were more receptive to black children's authors?

During the late sixties and early seventies, children's book publishers were opening up to blacks, but their interest in blacks disappeared rather quickly. It almost seemed like a particular day. It was as if the publishers got together and said, "Okay, enough of that."

In retrospect, those years when publishers welcomed blacks amounted to little more than a flash in the pan. Before then there was only Ezra Jack Keats doing picture books with black characters, and he wasn't even black. Since then, the number of black picture book authors is almost back to where it was before.

How would you typify the attitude of publishers toward blacks?

Nowadays the publishing industry deals with blacks as a special interest group. Every once in a while, they'll pay attention to blacks. They might do something to coincide with Martin Luther King Day, but they won't make an ongoing commitment. One birthday is fine, but they don't want to have a birthday party every day.

Some people argue that children's books by white authors that feature black characters should not be published or purchased. What's your reaction to this argument?

While it's true that white authors can't write from personal experience when they write about blacks, I think it's a mistake to prevent them from including black characters in their books. If they don't go ahead and do it, it means that children's books will have even less blacks in them, and that's not good for black kids or white kids. Ideally, I'd like to see more black images produced by black folks, but that doesn't preclude whites from writing about blacks.

How do you feel about the proliferation of picture books featuring African folktales?

Many of them are fine books, but I wish more of them had people instead of animals as the main characters. It's what I call the Brer Rabbit syndrome. I have nothing against animal stories, but we also need to have books with black people in them. It's much easier, however, to publish an African folktale about animals than a story about black people. The animal stories still sell. In fact, the best thing I could do for my career right now is publish a bunch of books like *Jumping Mouse* where the readers can't tell whether I'm black or white, but I won't. While I enjoyed working on *Jumping Mouse,* I prefer to do stories about people. I prefer to do stories in which black kids can see themselves.

Were you thinking along these lines when you entered the picture book field?

I really didn't know what the hell I was doing back then. You have to remember that I was just a teenager when I started doing picture books. I knew that my books were different from the books that I had read as a boy, but I didn't give much thought as to why. I simply wanted to create books that reflected my world. It wasn't until I got older that I started thinking about picture books in political terms.

Of all of your books, *My Special Best Words* aroused the most controversy. Did you anticipate this controversy when you were working on it?

When I wrote that book, I had been in the field for about five years, so I knew I was breaking taboos. In some ways, the book was a rebellion against all of our hang-ups about bodily functions. I decided to write a book that spoke to kids as biological beings, and one of the things that biological beings do is piss. So I included it in the book. The book is actually about my own kids who were preschoolers back then, and the events that happen in the book are the sorts of things that happen to most preschoolers.

Why is it that something as universal as toilet training can upset so many people?

Just because something is universal doesn't mean that it's not threatening. Artists often try to dig deep within themselves so that they can reach the point where their work becomes universal. They sometimes discover, though, that not everybody wants to go there. A lot of people don't want to deal with the things that are buried within them. And that's when they start to censor things. They don't move or change or grow.

There is another type of censorship that I'd like you to comment on, and that's the censorship of racist books.

The best way to deal with racist garbage in children's books is to provide kids with books that aren't racist. That's why I keep saying that we need more books about blacks. The other thing we need to do is talk to our kids about racist stereotypes. What we don't need to do is start burning books.

Some of the black picture book authors who got their start around the same time that you did are

no longer doing picture books. Do you intend to stay in the field?

I want to stay in it. There is still so much that needs to be done and so much that I want to do. Right now, for example, I'm working on black infant books. As far as I know, I'm the first person to do this. It's a delicious opportunity.

Some people ask me when I'm going to grow up and do adult books. But that's not how I see it. Creating picture books is a valid thing to do. You don't have to graduate from picture books to something else.

THE
PUBLISHERS
SPEAK

Richard W. Jackson

Shortly after Richard W. Jackson and Robert J. Verrone met in the mid-sixties, they began discussing the idea of becoming publishers of children's books. Both were already very familiar with the publishing world. Jackson had worked as an editor for several major publishing firms, and Verrone had administrative experience with Prentice-Hall. Their discussions resulted in the formation of Bradbury Press in 1968. It began as an imprint of Prentice-Hall, but in 1970 it became an independent press and remained so until 1982 when it became an affiliate of Macmillan. Jackson and Verrone's partnership lasted until Verrone's death in 1984. Jackson left Bradbury Press in 1986 and now directs Richard Jackson Books, an imprint of Orchard Books.

As a publisher of children's books, Jackson has played a significant role in the rise of what has come to be known as the new realism in children's literature. In his role as editor-and-chief at Bradbury Press, he encouraged authors to write honestly and not to be overly concerned about the taboos that children's authors had traditionally been expected to uphold. One of the first authors to benefit from Jackson's more open attitude was Judy Blume.

What was your first contact with Judy Blume?

Judy had seen Bradbury's first *New York Times* ad and discovered that our offices were in New Jersey. Well, she was in New Jersey and didn't like coming to New York, so it was the New Jersey connection that really drew us together. She sent us the manuscript of *Iggie's House,* and like other manuscripts, it sat around for a while. It was Bob who read it first, and he liked her use of dialog. I agreed, and we accepted it.

What was your initial response to *Are You There God? It's Me, Margaret?*

When Judy first talked to us about *Margaret,* we knew it had the potential to raise some hackles. After reading the manuscript, though, we felt it was deliciously honest, delicately done, and very tender. The book came out of Judy's own life and extraordinary memory of those things, such as menstruation, which were never discussed but were on every girl's mind. During the editorial process, which was very intense, we made no attempt to tone down Judy's openness.

In Judy's next "sexual" book, which was *Then Again, Maybe I Won't,* I encouraged her to be even more open. At one point, I suggested that boys experience erections quite often and sometimes at inopportune moments; it seemed to me that this was one of the things that Tony, the boy in the book, might experience. Judy went on to portray this experience accurately (and amusingly). As a result, though, the novel came to be viewed as a book about wet dreams and such. Well, that's foolishness because it's really about class clash, about conflicting social values.

How did the critics respond to these books when they first came out?

Margaret got a surprising reception. Some of the people we thought would not cotton to it were very responsive. We figured, though, that these people were mostly women responding to themselves as children. With *Then Again,* we thought we were really testing the waters because the women critics would be looking at boys, and boys, alas, are often seen as disgusting creatures. But—to my astonishment—many of the people who liked *Margaret* also liked *Then Again.* It has never sold quite as well as her other books, and the reason, I think, may be because there's a boy in the center of it.

When did you first become aware of attempts to censor her books?

I remember back in about 1975 I received several letters about *It's Not the End of the World,* but they were isolated complaints and usually related to language, such as the use of the word "bastard." Then letters started about *Blubber.* Some of these letters were also about language, but others complained that Judy never came right out and said that cruelty is wrong; rather, she simply said that cruelty exists and described what it feels like. But there is another reason why some adults get upset about *Blubber.* Judy makes a very unsettling point, and that is that some people practically invite cruelty because they are such drips. Judy says, at least by implication, that kids have a choice: They can drip through life, or they can stick up for themselves. Kids understand this, but it makes some adults uncomfortable because adults tend to grow sentimental about childhood. Children are *not* sentimental.

At what point did the sexual content of her books begin attracting the attention of censors?

It was around 1979 or '80. I started opening lots of letters about *Deenie*—and some of Judy's other books, too. I also remember a phone call from an angry father who began the conversation by asking, "Are you a Christian?" He then went on to say that he was upset about the use of the word "tits" in *Starring Sally J. Freedman as Herself.* I'm amazed how long it took the censors to respond. These books by Judy had existed for nearly a decade before the censors suddenly descended on them as if they had just leaped into the culture and could still be stamped out.

What specific charges did the letter writers make when they wrote to you about *Deenie?*

They often accused Judy of putting sexual material in the book simply to make it titillating. Some went so far as to call *Deenie* a how-to manual about masturbation. Well, Judy does mention masturbation, but that's not what the book is about; it's about self-image. The masturbation passages are integral to this theme. All kids have heard those myths about the terrible things that are supposed to happen to them if they masturbate, so it is natural for *Deenie* to wonder if masturbation might have something to do with her curvature of the spine. I agreed with Judy that Deenie needed to come to terms with this fear and learn that she did not get curvature of the spine for doing something that both Judy and I view as being completely natural. Of course, many fundamentalists do not view masturbation as natural.

Did these attacks have any effect on the editing of Blume's books?

I'm afraid they had a direct influence on the editing of *Tiger Eyes* in 1980. Judy included a brief passage in which she dealt with masturbation. I told her that she could leave the four lines in the book, but as her publisher I had to tell her these lines could become the focus of another controversy. This is not to say that I thought that the masturbation reference was inappropriate or psychologically unsound. Judy never makes mistakes about what is psychologically sound. I really did not think I was asking her to censor these lines, and she did agree to take them out.

Some of Blume's critics argue that the only reason kids like her books is because of the sexual passages. What do you think?

Some right-wing people say so, but the real reasons for the books' successes are, I think, not really related to sex. Kids like the books because in them the writer seems to disappear. In effect the child reader is listening to Margaret or any of the other narrators confide the story. There is apparently no adult guiding it. Adults do figure in the books, but they are not intrusive (and often they are positive and tenderhearted people). Judy thinks the books are popular because she emphasizes feelings. I guess we all have our own theories.

Do you think there is a relationship between her popularity and the censorship of her books?

Certainly. One of the things about the books that drives some people crazy *is* their popularity. The kids found Judy Blume. The kids, in other words, asserted a kind of power which drew the attention of the adult world to the existence of Judy Blume. Other writers who are equally good, equally skillful, and equally "dangerous" don't cause the same kind of waves simply because they are not as famous. The visibility of the target makes a difference.

Can you think of any other reasons why some people are so threatened by her books?

Well, I suspect that one of the underlying factors behind the censorship of Judy's books is the right's discomfort with some changes in our conceptions of what is right and wrong. They miss the days when there was a right and a wrong and that was it. Nowadays most of us still feel there is a right and a wrong, but deciding which and where is not so clear-cut. In the nineteenth century, kids generally knew how they were supposed to live their lives, but today they are faced with endless decisions, freedoms, alternatives. Judy's books recognize this fact. Through her books, Judy says, "It's your life. How are you going to live it?" That question is very troublesome to the Falwells who don't want their kids to think for themselves. Their desire to have complete control over their children is an outgrowth of the panic they must feel when confronted with the realities of modern times.

How are these broader changes reflected in the world of children's books?

When Bob and I founded Bradbury Press, we sensed that the children's book world had agreed upon a certain view of reality which did not correspond to ours. The reason for this is that children's books often were seen as an extension of moral education. In the old days, the kids in children's books, or at least the heroes, were not allowed to behave immorally. Bob and I objected to this attitude, but we were not the first to do so. It is hard to say exactly when the old approach to children's literature began to give way, but I see the publication of *Harriet the Spy* in the mid-sixties as something of a turning point. In *Harriet* we have a hero who was doing something immoral, and it is totally understandable. We love her, and we identify with her.

Children's books have changed, I suppose, because more and more of us are beginning to view children as not being radically different from adults in terms of emotions. One of Freud's lessons is that children, like adults, are bundles of a wide range of feelings. We are finally beginning to acknowledge, in fiction, children's sexuality, their feelings of loneliness and anger. I'm not sure why this change has occurred. Maybe it has something to do with our experience with wars. Whatever the reasons, our attitudes toward children have changed, and we can't ever go back—despite the efforts of the people on the right.

Phyllis J. Fogelman

Phyllis J. Fogelman has been involved in the editing and publishing of children's books since 1961. She began her career at Harper & Row, where she worked in the children's book department for five years. In 1966, she was asked to serve as editor-in-chief of Dial Books for Young Readers. She accepted the offer and has been there ever since. While retaining the position as editor-in-chief, she was also made publisher, and in 1987 became the first president of Dial Books for Young Readers. In her long career at Dial, she has become known as an innovative and highly principled publisher. She has, for example, made a strong commitment to publishing black authors and illustrators. She has also committed a considerable amount of time and energy to anticensorship work.

For almost five years Fogelman served on the Freedom-to-Read Committee of the Association of American Publishers. This committee consists of publishing executives who are concerned about First Amendment issues. The committee has its own legal counsel and is often involved in censorship cases that go to court. It also sponsors public programs and publishes and distributes several informative pamphlets. Copies of these pamphlets can be obtained by writing to the following address: Freedom-to-Read Committee, Association of American Publishers, 2005 Massachusetts Ave., N.W., Washington, DC 20036.

When did you begin to view censorship as a serious problem?

It's hard for me to remember a time when I didn't view it as a problem. I guess I first became concerned about censorship during the McCarthy years. In my twenty-five years in the publishing field, I've published a number of books that have involved censorship issues, and this has kept me acutely aware of the problem.

In 1981 I became a member of the Freedom-to-Read Committee of the Association of American Publishers. Soon after I joined the committee, I participated in a televised panel discussion on the issue of book banning. There were about twenty people on the panel, ranging from right-wing fundamentalists to left-of-center civil libertarians. Judy Blume and Kurt Vonnegut represented authors, and I represented trade book publishers. It was a very interesting experience that expanded my first hand knowledge of how procensorship groups operate.

What do you mean by that?

Well, it was the first time I had face-to-face discussions with the highly organized fundamentalist procensorship people. By sheer chance I had breakfast alone with the two representatives from the Moral Majority. Over the course of my conversation with these two men, I realized that we had more than political differences. I was there as a full-time publisher and editor who was taking a little time away from my job to speak out against censorship. They, on the other hand, were *doing* their job; they were executives of the Moral Majority who devoted almost all of their time to getting their organization's point of view across. That's what they were paid to do. In comparison to them, those of us on the other side almost looked like dilettantes. Although I was certainly aware of it before, at that point it became even clearer to me why the Moral Majority and other similar organizations have gained so much ground. They are by no means the majority, but they put a lot of money, time, and people into their campaigns, and that's why they wield so much power.

Of all the authors whom you have published, which one has been the most censored?

It has to be Norma Klein. The first of her books that we published was *Naomi in the Middle* in 1974, and I'm pretty sure it's the book that we've gotten the most complaints about since I've been with Dial. I knew when I accepted it that we would have censorship problems with it, but that didn't affect my view of the book. I felt then and I still feel that it's a warm family story and that the questions Naomi asks about sex are ones that kids really ask.

Another Klein book that we've gotten a lot of complaints about is *It's OK If You Don't Love Me,* which we published as an adult book. What I like about this book is that it presents sexuality as a normal impulse that we need not feel guilty about. I like this approach so much more than the old moralistic stories in which the girl always gets punished for being sexual. The book is often accused of promoting promiscuity, but it really doesn't.

Have you seen any changes in the types of books that attract the attention of censors?

In the seventies and early eighties most of the censorship letters received by publishers related to sexuality, but now censors are broadening their scope to include anything that seems even vaguely anti-Christian to them. For a number of fundamentalist groups, certain words are seen as red flags. If a book simply includes the words *devil* and *witch,* it's enough to cause these people to file a complaint.

We recently ran into a problem with a boxed set of miniature books called *The Little Box of Witches.* A major book club was interested in buying some of our boxed sets, but we lost the sale because they were loath to buy the set about the witches. They were afraid that it would offend their "conservative" members and their fear wasn't totally unreasonable. After all, *The Wonderful Wizard of Oz* came under attack in Tennessee because it was purported to portray witches in too positive a fashion.

I must say, though, that it's hard to come up with definite trends in the area of censorship. In my years in publishing I've noticed a certain randomness about the kinds of books that are censored or attacked. There are some titles that I expect to be criticized, but we also get letters of complaint about books that seem completely inoffensive. I once received a very angry letter about *Noisy Nora,* a charming picture book by Rosemary Wells. The story is about a middle child in a family of mice. As you would expect, Nora feels left out and tries to attract attention to herself. Well, the woman who wrote the letter said that the story rewards bad behavior and should not be given to children. She went on to add that all of Wells's books should be removed from the library. If a book as uncontroversial as *Noisy Nora* can come under attack, any book can. That's why we cannot afford to open up the Pandora's box of censorship. Once we say it's okay to censor certain books, none would be safe.

Some of the authors I've interviewed say that publishers are becoming more reluctant to publish

books that might arouse controversy. As a publisher, do you think this is true?

I can't speak for other publishers, but I don't think we are doing anything appreciably different now than before. What is different is that we are even more aware of the possible consequences of including certain things in books, and we do sometimes communicate this information to our authors. If, for example, someone has a wonderful book in which a character uses the term *damn* just once, we will ask the author if that one *damn* is essential and let him or her know that it may cause adverse criticism for the book. Frequent use of that or similar terms would, of course, clearly indicate the sort of character the author is trying to describe. But if the author feels that the single *damn* helps define the character, we certainly won't demand that the word be taken out, nor will we change our minds about publishing the book. I've always felt that the book belongs to the author. We can make suggestions, but ultimately it's the author's decision whether or not to take our suggestions.

When I interviewed John Steptoe he said that many publishers are no longer very interested in children's books by and about blacks. I know that this is not true for Dial, but is it true for other publishers?

I think there is something to his point. Publishers are influenced by what's going on in the country, by the general tenor of the times. And the fact is that our society has become less welcoming to minorities. In the seventies we used to hear about the backlash against the civil rights movement, but that term isn't even used anymore. The backlash attitude has settled

in; it's almost become a given. I'm sure that this has something
to do with why there are so few new black authors and illustrators working in the field these days.

Another reason we are seeing fewer minorities entering the children's book field has to do with cutbacks in
educational programs. Since Reagan came into office, it has
become harder to get scholarships and loans to go to college.
This helps explain why there are fewer blacks entering college
now than in the seventies. Well, it's harder to become a writer
or an illustrator without some college education. It isn't that
college is *necessary,* but if nothing else, it brings one into contact with the world of books, and that's essential for an aspiring
writer.

**Some children's book publishers claim that
they can't afford to publish books by or about blacks
because they lose money on them. Is there any legiti-
macy to this claim?**

It's been said that black books don't sell very well, but that
hasn't been our experience at Dial. Most of the books by black
authors that we publish sell very well. Of course, some of
these authors are major award winners—Tom Feelings,
Mildred Taylor, and Julius Lester are examples. But they were
not award winners when we started publishing them.

For the most part children's books by and about blacks
do better in the library market than in bookstores, but with the
emergence of stores that specialize in children's books, that's
starting to change. Another thing that is helping is the "Reading Rainbow" program on television. This program regularly
features books by and about blacks. Once a book has been on
the program, its sales usually increase. We need more of this
type of promotion of black books.

Do you see any differences in your role as a publisher and your role as an anticensorship activist?

As a publisher I'm very concerned about quality. I won't publish a book unless I'm convinced that it's a good book. When I'm fighting censorship attempts, though, I don't think in these terms. We need to defend all books, even those we dislike, if we want to make sure that the books we do like will not be taken off the shelves. If we pick and choose our fights and defend only those books that we love, we give up too much ground.

Stephen Roxburgh

Stephen Roxburgh has been the publisher of children's books for Farrar, Straus & Giroux since 1978. Before entering the publishing field, he taught children's literature at the State University of New York at Stony Brook, where he was also doing doctoral work.

Roxburgh played a central role in the controversy surrounding Margot Zemach's *Jake and Honeybunch Go to Heaven,* a picture book published by Farrar, Straus & Giroux in 1982. The book, which is based on black folklore, was criticized for being racist. When Roxburgh learned that this was the reason several libraries had refused to place the book in their collections, he came to the book's defense. He argued that librarians who refuse to purchase controversial books are engaging in a form of censorship.

When did you become concerned about the censorship of children's literature?

I was in academia before I was in publishing, and during that time I didn't take censorship too seriously. I knew of certain major cases, but back then I always regarded them with a great deal of humor. I found it amusing, for example, that *Stuart Little* had been censored for having a mouse who had been born to human parents. When I came to publishing, I stoped thinking of censorship as a joke, but it wasn't until I became embroiled in the *Jake and Honeybunch* controversy that I fully realized what a serious problem censorship really is.

How did the *Jake and Honeybunch* controversy come about?

Shortly after we published the book, our library services director and I attended the conference of the American Association of School Librarians. We overheard someone say that their library wasn't going to purchase the book. We asked why and were told that they were following the example of the library systems in San Francisco and Milwaukee. These systems, we were told, considered the book racist and refused to put it in their circulating collections. The person who told us this bit of information had not seen the book but assumed that the charge of racism must be true. When I got back to New York, I called someone from the San Francisco system and asked if what I heard was true. She said it was. I then wrote a letter in which I asked them to tell us formally what their objections were to the book. The nature of their response was distressing. The head of the San Francisco Library System wrote back to the president of Farrar, Straus & Giroux and said (and this is a quote that is clear in my memory), "If he," meaning me, "really doesn't know why we are not going to buy *Jake and*

Honeybunch, he is in the wrong line of work and should be selling banjos to minstrel troupes." We did not feel that this was an adequate or responsible answer. It seemed to us that the book was a victim of what is sometimes called preselection censorship. The best way to counter this type of censorship, we decided, was in a public forum, so we released the story to *The New York Times.* From there it got bigger and bigger.

We were accused of generating a controversy simply to sell books. In the children's book world, this charge makes no sense. If an adult book is banned in Boston, everybody wants to read it. But if there is a trace of controversy attached to a children's book, it's the kiss of death. Picture books, it must be kept in mind, are not bought by children. They're bought by adults, and for the most part, they are bought by public servants, such as school librarians, public librarians, and other representatives of institutions. Most people in these positions do not want to invite controversy.

When you went public with the story, did you feel you would succeed in changing people's minds about not buying the book?

No. We realized that it was a fight we could not win. Once a book has been tarred in that way, it simply can't be revived. So in some ways, the battle was lost before the forces were ever joined. But we still felt that it was necessary to defend the book as well as its author, Margot Zemach. As her publisher, we saw it as our responsibility to speak on her behalf. She, after all, is an individual, and individuals don't stand much of a chance against large institutions. While Farrar, Straus & Giroux is not exactly an institution, we certainly had the wherewithal to confront this in a public forum in a way that she would be hard-pressed to do.

How did the people who refused to buy the book respond when you brought up the question of censorship?

There were people who argued that this was not a case of censorship. They said that it's the job of librarians to select books for their libraries. We pointed out, though, that the reasons stated for not buying the book were contrary to the American Library Association's "Library Bill of Rights," which states that a variety of books and viewpoints should be made available.

I should point out that we are not talking about a poorly done book. This is a book by a Caldecott Medal winner. When it first came out, it received many favorable reviews. Nor is there any general agreement that it is racist. The American Black Book Writers Association said it wasn't and urged libraries to add it to their collections.

Roald Dahl, another author you publish, has also come under fire. How do you respond to the people who claim his books are too vulgar and violent?

I personally am not in the least bit offended by his earthy humor or his comic violence. It's clear to anyone who cares to look that he has a very good sense of what children find entertaining. Children love his books. They love his strong plots, his amusing characters, and his sense of humor. It's true that his books are violent, but his violence is always tempered with humor, and this, in my mind, mitigates the harshness of it.

The controversy surrounding Dahl is a classic instance of adults, who think they are the arbiters of good taste and decorum, trying to impose these qualities on children who are not particularly tasteful or decorous. Most children couldn't care less about adult conventions, and that's why they take great delight in Dahl's violations of these conventions. Adults, though, often find that violations of taste and decorum make them anxious and that's why they are uneasy with Dahl's books. In my experience, many adults have a tendency to become overly zealous when it comes to protecting children from certain books. They become righteous, and sometimes use their children as an excuse for their own intolerance. It's when adults see themselves as the protectors of innocent children that they can lose sight of other people's rights. They don't seem to realize the implications of saying, "No one else should look at this book because I've decided that it's harmful to children."

Many adults seem to think that children's books must be more than entertaining. Where did this idea come from?

It goes way back, and became clear in eighteenth-century educators' notions that books for children should be morally didactic. According to these notions, books are tools by which adults can influence children and, in so doing, shape the future. In other words, children's books are expected to help correct the behavior of individual children as well as the social problems of the culture into which they are born. While didacticism in children's books is nowhere near as bad as it used to be, this notion lingers on, and books that violate it still run the risk of encountering adult disapproval.

At what point does disapproval turn into censorship?

As I see it, censorship requires the involvement of institutions. I don't think individuals acting alone can really function as censors. They can register an opinion. They can say, "I don't like this book, I won't buy it, and I don't think other people should buy it." They can even write a letter to the publisher or the author and explain why they don't like it, but that isn't censorship. Censorship occurs when institutions or organizations take a stand against a book and exert their influence and power to limit the book's availability to the public.

From your perspective as a publisher, what are the most serious effects of the movement to censor children's books?

The effects that concern me the most are the ones that no one hears about. All too often, publishers, editors, authors, and illustrators are making decisions in anticipation of objections from some unknown and vaguely threatening other. Because of this, there are certain subjects, themes, actions, and words that are being screened out of books. Sometimes it's a conscious decision, but just as often it's made subconsciously. Whatever the case, the result is the same: controversial material is being eliminated or watered down.

The fear of controversy makes the people involved in producing children's books more and more conservative. This worries me since it's already a conservative field. It takes a long, long time for children's books to change, mainly because most adults don't pay much attention to the newer books. When they go into a bookstore in search of a children's book, they ask for *Black Beauty* or *Heidi*. It's not that they think these are the best books ever written; it's just that they're the only books that they can remember having read some twenty or thirty years ago. For all of these reasons, I've become convinced that the children's book world is fast becoming the most conservative world this side of banking.

THE
ANTI-
CENSORSHIP
ACTIVISTS
SPEAK

Judith F. Krug

Judith F. Krug is a leading figure in the American Library Association's (ALA) anticensorship campaign and has been for many years. Since 1967 she has directed the ALA's Office for Intellectual Freedom. She is also the executive director of the Freedom to Read Foundation. Krug frequently contributes articles about censorship to library and education journals and is the recipient of many awards for her anticensorship work, including the Harry Kalven Freedom of Expression Award, presented by the American Civil Liberties Union, and the Open Book Award, presented by the American Society of Journalists and Authors.

As director of the Office of Intellectual Freedom, Krug oversees the office's various services and activities. These include helping librarians resist censorship attempts, conducting educational programs for librarians and others concerned about censorship, and editing the bimonthly *Newsletter on Intellectual Freedom*. The *Newsletter* began publication in 1952 and has become one of the best sources of information about censorship attempts. It also provides comprehensive coverage of court cases and legislation concerning censorship. Subscription information can be obtained by writing to: Office for Intellectual Freedom, American Library Association, 50 E. Huron St., Chicago, IL 60611.

In the years that you have been involved in anticensorship work, what changes have you seen regarding the censorship of children's literature?

I started here in 1967, and while things have changed somewhat, they haven't changed quite as radically as people might imagine. The literature has changed substantially, but the public's reaction to it has been fairly constant. There always have been and probably always will be individuals who believe that children are innocent and who complain when they believe this innocence is being threatened. The nature of these complaints has not changed all that drastically. What has changed is the content of the books. Since the late sixties, children's books have become much more realistic. They not only deal with real-life problems, but they are also starting to explore the child's sense of reality. Judy Blume, of course, started the whole trend of writing about young people's problems as seen through young people's eyes and expressed in young people's language. One of the reasons she is so extremely popular with children and young adults is that she is able to get inside their world.

Why did these new trends in children's literature occur during this period?

I think changes in children's literature reflect broader societal changes. The civil rights movement, the antiwar movement, and the women's movement all led us to question age-old traditions and truisms. In keeping with the general spirit of the time—the questioning, the restlessness—some children's authors began to redefine children's literature.

In some ways, contemporary children's literature is based on a new value system, one in which the nuclear family is no longer the focal point. Less than half of today's families conform to the nuclear family model, and the old assumptions that helped to perpetuate the nuclear family are no longer taken for granted. We are living in a more open society, and authors like Judy Blume, Norma Klein, and Robert Cormier have taken advantage of this openness.

Given this new openness, why has the censorship of children's literature become such a serious problem in recent years?

Not everyone has come to terms with the social changes that have occurred over the last twenty years, and book censors are among them. These are people who can't cope with our new world, and they want to go back to the way it used to be. But the changes are too profound and too deep-seated to be turned back. That doesn't mean that I don't take the censors seriously; I do. The point is, though, that we can't lose sight of the broader picture. While I am not a historian, I read enough to know that the line of progress is not a steady line; it usually does some zigzagging along the way. I'm sure that the Reagan years will eventually be seen as a temporary zig in the line.

How would you describe the relationship between the Reagan administration and the proliferation of censorship cases that have occurred during his administration?

The same factors that led to the increase in censorship also led to the election of Reagan. In other words, Reagan and censorship do not have a cause and effect relationship. Rather, they are two effects of one basic set of causes. I don't believe that Reagan is personally responsible for all the censorship cases that have occurred during his administration. Reagan has an agenda, but taking books off library shelves probably isn't on it. What Reagan has done is create an environment that is conducive to censors, be they in or out of government. Thus, even though we have had more censorship pressures from the Reagan administration than any other administration in recent history, it is too much of a simplification to blame it all on Reagan. It is important to remember that the big increase in censorship started a year or so before Reagan was even elected.

What was it about the late seventies that caused people to begin attacking children's reading materials?

First of all, this was a period when the economy was not too healthy. If you trace the history of censorship, you'll find that when the economy goes down, censorship attempts go up. More importantly, however, this was a period when the political right was gaining momentum, and one of the first things that people on the right did was turn their attention to the schools and the materials that were taught in the schools. Historically, political movements have often focused on the schools, for schools deal with two of the most important subjects in our lives: our children and our money. This attention on the public schools resulted in a scrutiny of curricular materials and school library holdings.

Many of the leaders of the political right claim that they are speaking for the majority of Americans when they advocate the banning of books. How do you view this claim?

The complainers, the anti-intellectuals, the procensorship people are truly a minority. Jerry Falwell may make a lot of noise, but he really doesn't speak for the majority of Americans. In many ways, we can thumb our noses at them and say, "Who has time for this silliness?" In reality, though, it would be a mistake to thumb our noses at them because the damage they can do, even if it's short-term damage, will need to be repaired. If we ignore them now, it will only mean that in the future we will need to spend even more time, effort, and money to work our way out of this situation. I can assure you that it is very tiring to go back and refight the old battles.

Do you ever feel like just walking away from these battles?

Sometimes, but if you don't keep fighting, you run the risk of having the laws dealing with civil liberties, laws which provide us with an opportunity to seek a more open and just society, overturned or chipped away at. This chipping away process is what is happening to the First Amendment right now. I don't think that the Reagan administration or any other administration is going to take the First Amendment and throw it out like a loaf of stale bread. Instead, they chip away at the loaf. They make it smaller. They diminish its substance and its sustenance. Part of my job is to keep putting back those chips.

Another thing that keeps me going is the friendships that I have developed with some of the people whose books we're trying to protect. One result of the battle over Judy Blume's books, for example, is that she and I have gotten to know each other quite well. When defending her books, I feel like I'm defending a friend. That feeling will always sustain me no matter how many times I have to go to battle over her books.

Based on your experiences in these battles over Blume's books, what are the major reasons her books so often come under attack?

The kids like her, which automatically makes her suspect among some adults. She is also censored because she doesn't tack a moral onto the end of her books. When *Blubber* was attacked in a school system in Maryland, the mother complaining said, "The book doesn't have a moral. Blume doesn't say that it's not nice to pick on children in your class." Of course, the reason that she doesn't is that she trusts that her readers will come to that conclusion on their own. Judy is often accused of being amoral or immoral. In reality, though, she is a very moral person; it's just that her morals are different from the morals of her accusers.

One of the other problems that these people have with Judy Blume is that she deals with children's unhappiness and uncertainties, and these people don't want to acknowledge that children have such problems. I remember once riding in a limousine back from the airport with a fashionable woman from the North Shore. We started talking, and she brought up *Are You There God? It's Me, Margaret.* She said, "Judy Blume is terrible because she brings all of these problems to young people." And then she went on and on about how bad *Margaret* was because the character worries about her period. She was upset when she caught her thirteen-year-old daughter reading the book. "I don't want my daughter to worry about menstruation," she said. "I want it to be a wonderful experience." I asked her if she ever worried during her teenage years, and she replied, "Oh no, they were the best years of my life." Well, I was sitting there thinking about how miserable I felt when I was thirteen, and I had a tremendous amount of support from my family. I tried to imagine what it would be like to be this woman's daughter. How could you talk to your mother about your problems if your mother refuses to admit that problems even exist? It seems to me that such parents are essentially ignoring the needs of their children. Fortunately for the children, Judy Blume's books are helping to fulfill these needs that are not being met at home, and that might be why the parents feel so threatened by the books.

What role does the sexual content of her books play in the controversy surrounding Blume?

Of course, she is frequently accused of being too sexual, but I learned a long time ago that the charge of being too sexual is often a smoke screen. I learned this lesson during the controversy surrounding Joan Baez's autobiography, *Day Break,* back in the early seventies. There was one so-called dirty word in that book, and it is used in a humorous story about her preschool child who didn't know the meaning of the word and used it out of context. Well, the book was removed from libraries all over the country because of its sexual explicitness. It was clear to me, though, that this was not the real reason for the banning of her book. At that point, she was one of the leading figures in the fight against the Vietnam War, and her husband was in prison as a conscientious objector. These things upset some people, but it was considered unsophisticated to ban a book because of the author's political beliefs, so they used the dirty words argument. I can't tell you how many times I heard people say, "It's a filthy book." But what they really meant was that they objected to Joan Baez's beliefs and political stands. It's the same thing that happens in many of the attacks on Judy Blume. The people who say that Judy Blume is too sexual often dislike much more than the few sexual passages in her books, but they won't come out and say what they really mean.

How do you respond to the people who say that Judy Blume's books should not be in libraries because the books are not of a high literary quality?

To begin with, I disagree with their evaluation of her books, but even if I didn't I would argue that her books should be in the libraries. The responsibility of librarians is to make a wide range of books available from which patrons can make their selections. While I certainly believe that the literary classics should be in libraries, I don't believe that works of popular fiction should be excluded. Nor do I think that patrons should be discouraged from checking out works of popular fiction even if the patrons are children. Making judgments on patrons' selections is not part of our job. I realize that there are still some members of this profession who believe it is their responsibility to improve the literary tastes of the masses. It is as if they have taken on the proverbial white man's burden for the heathen. This is a role that librarians should avoid, for it quickly leads to censorship.

Leanne Katz

Leanne Katz has served as executive director of the National Coalition Against Censorship (NCAC) since the coalition came into being. In addition to her administrative duties, she edits NCAC's quarterly newsletter, *Censorship News,* and lectures and writes on a range of issues related to First Amendment rights. She has also taught a course on freedom of expression at Queens College of the City University of New York. In recognition of her work, the American Society of Journalists and Authors awarded her its Open Book Award in 1984.

Under Katz's leadership, NCAC has evolved into a broad-based coalition of national, nonprofit organizations, all of which are dedicated to fighting censorship. At its formation in 1974, NCAC (then known as the National Ad Hoc Committee Against Censorship) spoke for twenty-six participating organizations. It has since grown into an alliance of over forty organizations, including religious, educational, artistic, professional, labor, and civil rights groups. As part of its work, NCAC sponsors conferences and meetings, disseminates information about censorship attempts, and assists groups and individuals who are engaged in anticensorship activities. More information about NCAC can be obtained by writing to: National Coalition Against Censorship, 132 W. 43 St., New York, NY 10036.

When did you first become involved in anticensorship work?

Throughout my entire career, I've been a First Amendment junkie. Back in the fifties I worked for the ACLU and was deeply involved in academic freedom work at the time that McCarthyism was rampant. I also did much traditional anticensorship work.

My first real job was as an ACLU secretary beginning in about 1952. After four years—my office was the ACLU library where (after college) I got my education—they promoted me to the professional staff, where I worked for another eight years. I served as the liaison between the national staff and the ACLU's local affiliates on everything other than legal and financial matters. Then I stayed home for almost ten years and raised my kids. In 1974 I came back to First Amendment work, to staff the newly formed National Coalition Against Censorship.

In the years that you have been a part of the anticensorship movement, have you seen any major changes in Americans' attitudes toward censorship?

There are some differences between the censorship of the fifties and today's censorship movement. In the fifties, politics figured more prominently. A good deal of the censorship was targeted against books by leftist authors, such as Howard Fast. You don't see so much of that today. On the whole, though, I see more similarities than differences. The impulse to censor has always been with us. The certainty of many people that they know what's best for everyone else is always with us. In fact, we all have this impulse although we may not recognize it as an impulse to censor.

You mentioned that in the fifties books by leftist authors were censored. What sort of books are most frequently censored today?

Practically all of the censorship litigation in the past decade relates to censorship in educational settings. These cases don't always involve children's books, but they all deal with books for students. The focus is often on textbooks or the standard novels that are read in high school.

Can you make any generalizations about why these books have come under attack?

Well, there are lots of reasons, but the most common one is the sexual content of the books. A great number of the people who want to ban books believe that sex is only for procreation. Period. And that's the beginning and the end of what they want their kids to know about sexuality. Now this attitude doesn't do much to guide the normal growing child. But from *their* point of view, it provides the child with all the guidance that he or she needs. If nothing else, it instills guilt, which they see as desirable.

It's easy to say that these people simply do not want their kids to read about sex, but I don't think that this is the only reason they want to ban books by such authors as Judy Blume and Norma Klein. The people who are most active among the censors are frightened by more than sex; they are frightened by uncertainties, by unrest, by anything that upsets their universe. This basic insecurity is typical of many strong adherents to rigid belief systems. Such people want to feel that their system provides all the correct answers to life's questions. Other answers, other ways of looking at the world, seem to threaten them to a remarkable degree.

It's tempting to say that this insecurity is tied to lack of education, or to limited opportunities for intellectual achievement. And certainly many of these people are poorly educated, but this isn't true of all of them. We know that some of the leading fundamentalists are quite smart and well educated. So why are they so afraid of ideas? I think it has something to do with power. The leaders fear that they will lose their authority if their followers have access to a lot of other ideas.

Would you say that this concern about maintaining authority affects the way in which fundamentalists raise their children?

Certainly. Fundamentalists and other parents who ascribe to the rigid belief systems believe they must shelter their children from diverse ideas or they may lose control over them. The Amish offer a fascinating example of this pattern. I can understand why the Amish prohibit their kids from being formally educated beyond a certain age. They are quite correct in thinking that they will lose them to the larger culture if they are allowed to continue as part of that culture. I sympathize with them, and part of me feels that they have a religious right to isolate their children. But another part of me asks, "What about the kids' rights?" Our society does not give a great deal of thought to that question. For the most part, kids just seem to be considered the property of their parents.

Do you think that the First Amendment should apply to children?

There is no question in my mind that kids should have at least some First Amendment rights. I also believe that having access to a variety of books, ideas, and the like is very good for the intellectual and psychological development of children. Now I won't say that no one was ever harmed by an idea, but I know we take far greater risks when we deny children access to ideas than we do when we expose them to ideas. Perhaps it's not surprising that the courts have been quite equivocal about the First Amendment rights of children. One of the reasons for this is that parents' rights and kids' rights can easily conflict. When I'm asked, I say that a parent may have the right to restrict his or her own child's reading materials, but the parent does not have the right to place restrictions on other parents' children. Every time I say that, though, I'm aware that there's an important question—when can a young person make independent decisions?—that's being ignored.

What is the fundamentalists' stand on this issue?

They generally argue that kids don't have any First Amendment rights. And they don't just mean young children; they mean teenagers, even seventeen- and eighteen-year-olds. In a recent case in California, parents of eighteen-year-old high school students argued that they should still have complete control over what their kids read. Many such people tend to feel that teenagers should not be allowed to make any of their own decisions, that they should not be treated as adults, that they should not be in any way exempt from parental authority.

Why do they mistrust their children so much?

It's not so much that they mistrust children. They essentially have little faith in *anyone's* ability to make good decisions, no matter how old the person is. The idea that our choices might be better as our freedom increases is totally alien to them. This is a basic difference between those who support restrictions and those of us who oppose censorship. We believe that even if people are not perfectible, even if we are often wrong and often mediocre or even unethical, there is still no better way to improve our lot than to keep trying to give people the means, the information, on which to base good choices, good individual decisions.

Another thing that separates censors from us is their belief that there is only one way to *interpret* words or ideas. The religious right does not appreciate ambiguity. In fact, I think it's fair to say that they simply can't tolerate it. This intolerance of ambiguity makes life simple for them. It gives them a sense of moral and intellectual certainty that I find deeply troubling.

Do you think their children are put off by this attitude?

I'm sure that some children of fundamentalists feel stifled by their parents' rigidity, but others adapt easily to this way of being raised. Children are often fragile and tend to like easy answers to difficult questions. Some of the private Christian schools capitalize on this. They require kids to memorize a whole series of answers to life's questions. Many children—and many adults—find it very hard to resist this type of indoctrination.

Don't these people realize that this approach to child rearing can impede their children's psychological development?

We have to keep in mind that they care much more about their children's spiritual development than their psychological development. To them the crucial matter is that their children not stray spiritually.

How have children's reading materials been affected by the fundamentalists' censorship campaigns?

I don't think the fundamentalists have had a major impact on the publishing and marketing of children's books. Blume's books, for example, have not become less popular because they are so often censored. But I do think the fundamentalists have had a significant impact in the textbook field. Many of us have been laughing at the fundamentalists ever since the Scopes trial, but while we've been laughing, they've been getting the science books changed. There probably isn't a legitimate scientist around who isn't gravely concerned about the deteriorating quality of science textbooks. I think the fundamentalists have had a very damaging effect on the teaching of science in this country.

Another area where the fundamentalists have had an impact is in school libraries. School librarians and, to a lesser extent, public librarians are becoming more and more cautious about buying books by certain authors or about certain subjects.

What concerns you the most about the current censorship movement?

I'm not greatly concerned about the occasional parent who gets upset about a particular book. I worry much more about people who become obsessed with banning books. It's not so hard to understand the irate parent, but the obsessive censor is another matter. It is hard to get inside the mind of the true believer, the obsessed crusader. These people see themselves as being personally responsible for stamping out a perceived evil, an evil that they feel is lurking everywhere, and they feel they must make other people conform to their warnings and beliefs. Yet when you read their books or listen to their speeches, you detect a disturbing sense of hatred, a sense of underlying violence. It's difficult to avoid the recognition that these people are extremists. For them the First Amendment means little. And yet the First Amendment protects extremists, so there is something in me that always feels a little protective of these people. I'm glad there are people who are obsessed with causes, and I admire their passion. Even though they may be the embodiment of intolerance, I think we need to defend their right to express their views. But at the same time, we cannot allow them to take away our First Amendment rights. It's a dynamic balance, and we have to work to keep it that way.

Barbara Parker

In the late seventies, Barbara Parker became concerned about the impact of censorship on the public schools. She was especially worried about Mel and Norma Gabler's efforts to censor the textbooks used by the school systems in Texas. She decided to conduct a lengthy interview with them in their home in Longview, Texas. The resulting article appeared in the June 1979 issue of *American School Board Journal.* This article won several journalism awards and helped establish Parker as an expert on this aspect of censorship. In 1982 she joined the anticensorship organization People for the American Way and became the director of its National Schools and Library Project, later renamed the Freedom to Learn Project. While holding this position, she helped change the textbook selection process in Texas, published articles on censorship, appeared on several television programs, and was the coauthor of *Protecting the Freedom to Learn: A Citizen's Guide.* Now operating a public relations consulting firm, Parker continues to write and speak on the topic of censorship.

People for the American Way continues to fight against the censorship of curricular materials. To make the public aware of this problem, it has produced the video presentation "Public Schools under Attack," copies of which are available for purchase. The organization also provides financial support to schools that are involved in court cases related to censorship. More information about its activities can be obtained by writing to: People for the American Way, 2000 M St., N.W., Washington, DC 20036.

How did People for the American Way come into existence?

Back in 1980, Norman Lear was thinking about doing a television series based on television evangelists. He started watching their programs and decided they were no laughing matter. He became very concerned by what he was seeing and hearing. It upset him when he heard these people claim that there is only one Christian way to vote, only one Christian way to think, only one American way to think. He got in touch with a lot of clergy and other influential people who shared his concerns. Together they prepared a sixty-second television spot that ended with a tag line that said People for the American Way and gave a post office box. Thousands of people wrote to this address, and it was out of this activity that the organization emerged. Essentially, it is an organization that was founded to protect constitutional freedoms.

What role have you played in the organization?

One of our program areas since 1981 has been to protect the freedom to learn in public schools and libraries across the country, and that's the area that I've worked in since joining the organization in 1982. One of my first projects was putting together a resource book called *Protecting the Freedom to Learn: A Citizen's Guide*. Around the same time, we started working to change the textbook adoption process in Texas. We chose Texas for two reasons: one, it is the single largest purchaser of textbooks and is therefore able to dominate the market; and two, it is the home base of Norma and Mel Gabler, and at that point they were practically dictating the types of textbooks that the state used. We conducted a grass-roots campaign. Many Texans joined us, and together we succeeded in changing the adoption process. Since then we have worked with thousands of teachers and parents who wish to preserve the educational integrity of the public schools. We have also made countless appearances on television and radio programs.

How have the news media responded to the censorship problem?

We have succeeded in getting a good deal of publicity largely because we have been able to get things done. If you accomplish things, the media are often willing to give you coverage as long as the issue is sexy enough. But the level of publicity varies depending on whether or not censorship is seen as a hot topic or what kind of news day it is. One problem is that censorship has become so common that it is sometimes seen as old news.

How do you respond to the people who say that the best way to deal with censors is just to ignore them?

While I certainly don't think that book censors speak for the majority of the population, I believe it is dangerous to ignore them or dismiss them as a bunch of kooks. They are making their voices heard at school board meetings and other forums, and unless we also make our views known they just might win, just as they recently did in Tennessee and Alabama. School boards need to know that many of us still feel that children should be exposed to a variety of ideas and be encouraged to question and think for themselves.

Too many people on our side of the censorship issue say, "Well, as long as the book is available in the public library, it's not worth making a big fuss if it's banned from the school library." Or they'll say, "There have always been people who want to ban books, so what's the use fighting it." We can't afford to give up the little battles so easily. We can't afford to stand by and watch our First Amendment rights gradually erode away.

Do you feel that the academic community has taken a strong enough stand against censorship?

Not really. The academic community professes to be against censorship, but it has often been quite silent when it comes to the banning of certain titles, especially those by young adult authors such as Judy Blume. There seems to be a kind of blind spot involved in their interpretation of the First Amendment. Several years ago we sponsored a luncheon during Banned Book Week, and we had a panel of speakers which included a student, a librarian, a bookseller, and an English teacher. I distinctly remember the English teacher saying that he would not speak up against the banning of a Judy Blume book, but if it were *The Catcher in the Rye* or *Huckleberry Finn,* he would fight it to the end. I think this kind of snobbery is misguided.

What do you say to the academics who refuse to defend Blume's books because they feel that the books lack literary merit?

I would not call all of Judy's books intellectual, but that doesn't mean that they don't have literary merit. Not only have her books stood the test of time, but they speak to children in a way that few books can. I know this from my own daughter. When she was around thirteen or fourteen, Judy Blume was one of her favorite authors. She found meaning and pleasure in Blume's books, and in my mind that qualifies the books as literature.

Why are Blume's books so frequently censored?

One of the reasons why authors such as Judy Blume and Norma Klein so often come under attack is that they write about aspects of reality that make many parents uncomfortable. In a sense, these parents would prefer for reality not to exist, and one way for them to try to make reality go away, at least in their own minds, is not to allow their children to have access to printed material that affirms that reality. In a self-deluding sort of way, they are trying to make all the "bad" things in the world simply disappear. They somehow feel that things like premarital sex will not occur if kids never read about it. It's the same with divorce, drugs, and other issues. Of course, these problems existed long before they were addressed in children's literature. When I was growing up in the fifties, nobody wrote children's books about sex, but teenage girls still got pregnant.

How are children viewed by the people who want to ban these books?

In many ways, the book censors want to return to a Victorian view of childhood, especially as it relates to sexuality. They try to do this by never letting their kids read anything that mentions sex, by never discussing sexuality with their kids, by strictly monitoring what their kids watch on television, and by putting their kids in fundamentalist academies where such topics are never brought up. By trying to turn the clock back, they end up making it very difficult for their kids to adjust to the real world.

What, besides sexuality, do the book censors want to protect their children from?

The fundamentalists feel that children should not read books that deal with confusion and uncertainty. They disapprove of stories in which characters wrestle with moral decisions or wonder about the meaning of life. This attitude also causes them to object to certain textbooks. A few years ago, for example, Norma Gabler, the textbook censor from Texas, wanted to delete a section from a health textbook because the section dealt with worrying. She argued that it is wrong to worry, that worrying is a sin. As far as she is concerned, children have no need to worry about whether something is right or wrong. They just need to ask their parents or their minister.

People like Norma Gabler and Phyllis Schlafly have a ready set of answers for any question. They have this little chart in their minds that says X, Y, and Z are wrong and A, B, and C are right. I once did a Phil Donahue show with Phyllis Schlafly during which she criticized a book because it contained a character who told a lie. When Donahue asked her if it would ever be right to lie, she practically became apoplectic and said, "No! Lying is Evil!" He asked her if she were in Hitler's Germany and the Nazis asked her where Anne Frank was hiding, would she tell the truth. She responded by screaming, "No! Lying is Evil!" Now, to my way of thinking, this is not the sign of a caring person or a thinking person.

Can you say a bit more about your overall impressions of the procensorship people whom you have met?

A person I have had frequent contact with is Phyllis Schlafly. We have been interviewed together on numerous occasions.

Often before the interviews we were virtually locked up together in little studios for forty-five minutes or so. I would try to make conversation with her, but it was practically impossible. She was always very tense and humorless. She seemed like a keg of dynamite that would explode if she laughed or admitted self-doubts.

I have also spent quite a lot of time with Norma and Mel Gabler. In 1979 I visited them for two days in their home in Texas. At that point, I was a journalist, and I was working on a story about their textbook crusade. It was the most frustrating forty-eight hours I have ever experienced. They refused to go into depth on any issue. I'd try to pursue a line of reasoning with them, but they would just keep going back to the same simple answers over and over.

What role does this type of simplistic reasoning play in their campaign against public education?

The fundamentalists' desire for easy answers has led many of them to use the schools as scapegoats. They argue that all of the things they don't like about our society have been caused by a group of well-organized secular humanists who have somehow taken over the public schools. They seem to believe that if they can just rid the schools of secular humanism, then all of society's troubles will quickly disappear. The problem will be nipped in the bud. Of course, this line of reasoning makes little sense, but the fundamentalists find it attractive because it makes the schools a convenient target.

What exactly do the fundamentalists mean when they say secular humanism?

Secular humanism is a catchall phrase that is almost impossible to define precisely. I have often said that trying to define it is like trying to nail Jell-O to a tree. The television evangelists claim that secular humanism is some kind of organized religion that is based on a nonbelief in God, which is something of a contradiction in terms. Essentially, the people who created the term and have perpetuated its use are the only ones who can define it, and they apply it to anything they find objectionable. It has been used to condemn science textbooks, *The Diary of Anne Frank, The Catcher in the Rye,* practically everything by Judy Blume and Norma Klein, and countless other books. In many ways, the whole idea of secular humanism is a great hoax, but it has caught on with the far right. Lots of people now think that the term "humanism" is a dirty word.

There is an underlying anti-intellectualism involved in the attacks on humanism. Fundamentalists feel that humanism puts too much emphasis on the human intellect, on human accomplishments. Many fundamentalists are quite suspicious of anything that is intellectual, artistic, or literary.

Would you say that most book banners share these suspicions?

I am certain of it. These people couldn't care less about protecting ideas or literature. Books are not the sort of things that they appreciate. Indeed, most of the people who file complaints against books have not actually read the books that they want banned. From the vast far right censorship network, they get lists of "dirty" books along with copies of two or three paragraphs from the books, and they base their judgments on this. That's how they came to the conclusion that Judy Blume's *Deenie* is a book about masturbation. Not only do these people not read the books for themselves, but they tend not to think for themselves. They follow orders, and that's what their leaders expect from them. It is militaristic behavior. Jerry

Falwell calls his Liberty Baptist College a boot camp for the Lord—you don't ask questions. This antiliterature bias relates to another major concern of mine, which is illiteracy. I believe that kids not only need to know how to read, but we need to help them to develop a desire to read. I sometimes wonder what's the point to being able to read if it's an option that's never taken. If we want our kids to choose a book over television, we need to provide them with books that they like. That's how one cultivates a desire to read. But, as is so often the case, the very books that kids like are ones that the censors want banned. This is why I feel that the censors are not only tampering with our constitutional rights, but they are also exacerbating the problem of illiteracy.

Amy A. McClure

Amy A. McClure taught in public schools for ten years as a classroom teacher, reading specialist, and coordinator of a program for gifted children. During this period, she became interested in censorship due to her awareness of the increasing number of incidents throughout the state of Ohio. This interest led her to chair the State Intellectual Freedom Committee for the Ohio International Reading Association (IRA) and to become a member of IRA's National Intellectual Freedom Committee. She is currently on the faculty of Ohio Wesleyan University where she teaches courses in reading and children's literature, supervises student teachers, and directs the university's honors program.

Since 1982, she has edited a column on censorship for the *Children's Literature Association Quarterly*. The column has examined a variety of topics, including general censorship trends, sexual and racial biases of censors, historical trends, and legal issues. The column is only one part of the Children's Literature Association's campaign against censorship. The association went on record against censorship in 1981, and since then it has often sponsored sessions on censorship at its annual conferences. More information about the association can be obtained by writing to: Children's Literature Association, 210 Education, Purdue University, West Lafayette, IN 47907.

How would you describe a typical censor?

I'm not sure there is a typical censor. One of the few things that they have in common is that they never call themselves censors. They see themselves more as saviors than censors. That's as true of the left as it is of the right. For example, I once gave a talk about children's literature, and I commented on the sexism in some children's books. Afterwards, a woman came up and said that she agreed with me and that she was planning to pull a certain sexist book off the shelves. I stopped her and said, "Wait a minute. Do you want to become a censor?" But she didn't see it that way. Censors frequently fail to see themselves for who they really are.

Another thing that censors have in common is a similar way of reacting to issues that they find objectionable. At least where their children are concerned, there are certain issues, sexuality being among them, that they simply do not want their children to read about. If a book just acknowledges the existence of sexuality, it's enough to cause some people to want to ban the book. They argue that sexuality is such a private issue that it should not be addressed in any forum outside of carefully controlled family discussions. At least that's their public position. I think there may sometimes be hidden reasons why they object to the acknowledgment of sexuality which probably has something to do with an uncomfortableness with their own sexuality. When dealing with censors, you need to distinguish between their public reasons and their hidden reasons. The public reasons are what they say to gather the broadest base of support for their positions. The private ones are often quite different.

Censors often say that they are only trying to prevent their children from being corrupted. Why do they believe that books have the power to corrupt children?

I'm afraid that some of the things that English teachers did in the past are now coming back to haunt us. For a long time, we tried to persuade people to read by making the rather romantic argument that reading a single book could radically change a person's life. Of course, we meant for the better. The censors argue, though, that if a single book can change a person's life for the better, then it can also change it for the worse. This helps explain why they look skeptical when we say that books alone cannot ruin children. It sounds like we are contradicting ourselves.

Are there any other ways that we seem to contradict ourselves?

Another apparent contradiction involves selection. It would be very easy for those of us who work in schools or libraries to justify our own censorship under the guise of selection. We have to be careful our own biases don't guide the selection process. But really we do have to have some kind of selection process. It's impossible to buy every book available. Even if we had unlimited financial resources, there is just not enough time. As teachers and librarians, we have to be selective as to what we're going to use, but we should make sure that our selections represent a variety of viewpoints, and are designed to provide balance in the collection. Ideally, selection is an inclusive process, whereas censorship is an exclusive process. I realize, though, that the line between the two is very fine. Certainly, our own personal biases can affect our selections. I think that the professional training that teachers and librarians go through helps correct this problem by making us aware of these biases so that we can rise above them, but I hope I'm not deluding myself.

What is the most common mistake that anticensorship people make when they are trying to resist a censorship attempt?

As I see it, one common mistake is to defend a book entirely on its literary merits. If you try to stop censorship by stressing the high literary quality of individual books, you are probably going to lose the battle. Responses to literature are so individual in nature that it is nearly impossible to arrive at a complete consensus about a particular book. For almost any title that you can name, there are going to be people who feel it is of high literary quality and others who feel it is trash.

In the end, it's better to take a more global approach to the problem. Instead of defending a particular book, you should stand up for all books, even if you don't especially care for some of them. I think this is especially important in the area of children's literature. There are some commonly censored children's books that are loved by children but disliked by many adults. If we don't defend these books, who will?

Why do children and adults so often disagree over what constitutes a good children's book?

It's often because they are looking for different things when they pick up a children's book. The children want to be entertained. They want a vicarious introduction to how people live and how people think so they can develop a better sense of themselves and the human experience. However, they are not as concerned about literary quality as adults. They certainly don't automatically give much thought to characterization and themes unless led to such reflections by adults. I know I didn't when I was a kid. I read all of the time, but I read for enjoyment. Most adults can understand this, but they also want children's books to be uplifting. They want children to be exposed to superior writing. They want children to experience books that take them beyond where they are. In some cases, adults want children to read books that help inculcate particular societal values. There are some children's books that succeed in pleasing both children and adults; *Charlotte's Web* is an example that immediately comes to mind. Perhaps that's why it's often called a classic.

What does it take for a children's book to be called a classic?

One of the criteria we commonly use to define a classic or, at least, a good children's book, is whether or not it appeals to adults as well as children. We often assume that a good children's book discusses a basic human truth in such a way that all generations will enjoy it. However, I think there is such a thing as a good children's book or "classic" that adults might not like. To insist that adults have to like a children's book to make it a good book is a little egotistical on our part.

As we've learned from the reader response theorists, our individual experiences and perceptions affect our responses to literature. Since children's experiences and perceptions are quite different from adults', it stands to reason that there will be certain books that children respond enthusiastically to but which don't elicit such responses from adults. By the same token, I think there are some children's books that really appeal much more to adults than to children. Thus, I often define a classic as a book which has stood the test of time; kept alive from one generation to the next through enthusiastic endorsement.

Why do many adults find some children's books so appealing?

For some adults, children's books can evoke feelings from a simpler time in their lives. They enjoy the happy resolution at the end which is almost invariable in children's books, though not always in adolescent books. They might also enjoy the simplicity and the directness of the plots. Much of the adult literature published today is pessimistic, and that bothers some adult readers. Maybe children's books offer them a little more hope and optimism as well as the opportunity to resavor some simple truths.

How would you compare the censorship of children's literature to the censorship of textbooks?

The two pretty much mirror each other, but the censorship of textbooks tends to be more organized and on a bigger scale. In some states, the textbook adoption process is very centralized. One group can decide what books will be used throughout the entire state. When the stakes are that big, the lobbying process becomes intense.

I'm most familiar with the conflicts over the reading books used in the elementary schools. One issue that comes up most frequently with these books is the portrayal of so-called traditional values. Many of the basal readers have been accused of being antifamily and anti-American. Let me give you some specific examples. In some of the basal reader stories, children help their parents solve problems. This supposedly undermines parental authority, according to objectors. There was another story about a Chinese immigrant family who still felt ties to China. This was supposedly anti-American. There are other reasons why basal readers have been attacked. Some people have tried to ban them because they portray women too traditionally. In contrast, Phyllis Schlafly and her Eagle Forum say the books should be banned because they contain too many career women. Even nutritionists have gotten in on the act.

They say there are too many references to cake and candy. Again, it's the same situation of personal biases influencing the desire to change public policy.

Why do textbook publishers so frequently give in to the censors?

One of the reasons textbook publishers are so susceptible to censorship pressures has to do with the economics of the publishing industry. The publishers of Blume's and Klein's books often sell their books directly to children, so they can afford to ignore the demands of censors. Textbook publishers, though, sell only to school systems. Consequently, if a major school system refuses to buy a certain textbook unless the publisher makes a change, the publisher is inclined to make the change. There is just too much money involved.

Do you deal with censorship in your children's literature classes?

Certainly. I have found, however, that if I have a class discussion about censorship, we just end up agreeing that censorship is bad. We don't get into the underlying issues or come to any better understanding of the parents' concerns. The most helpful thing that I've done with my students is to stage a debate. I have some of them assume the role of angry parents and some of them assume the role of school officials. The ones who pretend they're the parents find it very difficult because it's so alien to the way most college-age students think. But it is important for them to try to understand the perspective of the other side. Having the debate brings out all the different sides and helps the students really think through the issues.

Another thing I do when we are discussing a book that

has been attacked is say, "This book has been censored. Can you figure out why?" I remember doing that with William Steig's *Sylvester and the Magic Pebble.* It took my students a long time to figure out that it was because the police were portrayed as pigs. This is true for many other books we discuss.

Have you experienced any other problems in any of your anticensorship activities?

Yes. Sometimes I get the feeling that the only people who are listening to us are the people who already agree with us. I once did a radio talk show in which we were all vehemently anticensor, and we were waiting for the onslaught of calls from the fundamentalists. But all we got were calls from anticensorship people. I'm afraid, in other words, that we are simply preaching to the converted.

Have you seen any positive developments during the time that you've been involved in anticensorship work?

I've seen a major change in how schools and libraries deal with censorship problems. Back in the late seventies, principals and school board members often panicked when faced with complaints about books. In an attempt to avoid confrontations, they'd make quick and arbitrary decisions. They'd tell the teacher or the school librarian, "Take this book away before we get into any more trouble." The problem with this tactic was that it often encouraged more censorship. Parents felt that all they needed to do to ban a book was make a phone call.

Today school and library officials have become much

more adept at dealing with censorship pressures. Instead of panicking, they are taking a more organized and constructive approach. When a parent comes in with a complaint, they talk with the person. If the problem can't be worked out through a discussion, the parent is asked to fill out a form or is sometimes given a chance to speak before a school board meeting. The process is much more formal and organized than it used to be, and this tends to lead to fairer and more rational decisions.

Timothy B. Dyk

Timothy B. Dyk graduated from Harvard Law School in 1961, after which he served as a law clerk to several justices of the United States Supreme Court, including Chief Justice Warren. In 1964 he began working for Wilmer, Cutler & Pickering, a Washington, D.C., law firm, and became a partner in 1969. Dyk is a specialist in First Amendment law and has taught courses on the subject at the law schools of Georgetown University, the University of Virginia, and Yale University. He is also on the board of directors for People for the American Way.

Among the censorship cases that Dyk has participated in, *Mozert v. Public Schools* is one of the most important. It concerns several fundamentalist parents from Hawkins County, Tennessee, who took their local school board to court over a conflict about the use of certain textbooks. The parents wanted their children to be dismissed from class whenever the books were used; they claimed that the books are "anti-Christian." In October 1986, U.S. District Court Judge Hull ruled in favor of the parents. Several months later, another case involving textbooks reached the courts. A group of parents from Alabama sought to ban many textbooks from the public schools on the grounds that they advocate the "religion of secular humanism." William Brevard Hand, the judge hearing the case, sided with the parents. Both of these cases were appealed, and in August 1987 the original decisions were overruled by the Circuit Courts of Appeals. However, the plaintiffs in each case plan to appeal to the Supreme Court.

It should be pointed out that this interview took place before Judge Hull's and Judge Hand's rulings were reversed.

How did you get involved in the Mozert case?

I have been working in the First Amendment area for a while, but most of my previous work was in the free press area, especially as it relates to the regulation of broadcasters. I came into contact with People for the American Way and its then president, Anthony Podesta. I told Tony that I was interested in becoming involved in some of their cases dealing with religious issues, so when the Mozert case came up, Tony contacted me.

What role do religious issues usually play in censorship cases?

These cases have generally involved either the establishment clause of the Constitution or the free exercise clause. The establishment clause, of course, is the clause that prevents the state from founding or backing a religion, while the free exercise clause guarantees people the right to freely exercise their religion. In this country, going back for many decades, there have been concerns about the teaching of religious dogma in the public schools and the tailoring of the public school curriculum to serve religious interests. The first major case involving this issue was the famous Scopes trial in the 1920s where a public school teacher was criminally convicted for teaching evolution in violation of state law. It was not until 1968 that the Supreme Court finally decided the question at the heart of the Scopes trial. In *Epperson v. Arkansas,* the Court ruled that Arkansas could not prohibit the teaching of evolution because to do so was a violation of the establishment clause. This year in the *Edwards* case the Supreme Court held that Louisiana could not require that equal time be given to the teaching of creationism if evolution was taught. Recently some fundamentalists have claimed that the teaching in the public schools establishes a religion they call secular humanism. Many fundamentalists believe that secular humanism is a religion and that the schools, by teaching humanistic doctrines, are in effect teaching a religion. That is the issue in the recent case in Alabama.

In addition to the establishment clause cases, the Supreme Court has also grappled with free exercise cases in the public schools, for example, holding that children cannot be made to salute the flag or, in the case of the Amish, be made to attend public school after the eighth grade. Currently there is the Mozert case in Tennessee. The plaintiffs are claiming that the reading books used by the Hawkins County schools in grades one through eight violate their free exercise rights because the books include material that they find religiously objectionable. Among the broad range of things that they object to are such classics as *The Wonderful Wizard of Oz* and *The Diary of Anne Frank.*

In any of these cases, has there been a conflict between children's rights and parents' rights?

In most of these cases, it has just been assumed that the parents and their children share the same views. The one time the Supreme Court considered a case that suggested a possible conflict between the rights of parents and the rights of children was *Wisconsin v. Yoder,* which was decided in the early seventies. In this case, the question was raised whether Amish parents have the right to insist that their children stop attending school after the eighth grade. The state of Wisconsin was requiring that the children go to high school, but the parents objected to that because they wanted their children to grow up in the Amish faith and they felt that attending high school was a threat to that. I don't think anyone in that case thought that there was any difference between the parents' beliefs and the children's beliefs, but Justice Douglas was still concerned. He said that allowing the parents to take their children out of school was in effect denying the children the education that they would need to survive in the modern world. Without a high school education, the children could not make their own choice as to whether to grow up to be Amish or to grow up to be something else.

Justice Douglas made an important point. It doesn't necessarily depend on proving that individual children have differences with their parents. What's important is that children not be deprived of the opportunity to make choices that are different from their parents' choices.

Does the government have the legal authority to ensure that children receive a good education?

This has been an area of conflict for a long time. In the twenties, the Supreme Court said that the state cannot require children to attend the state school system. The right to attend private schools is one that everyone can exercise whether or not he has religious objections to the public school curriculum. The question arises, though, as to what kind of supervision the state can give to the religious schools to ensure that the students attending these schools are well educated. That's an active area of litigation right now, so we don't have any final answer to it.

The Mozert case very starkly raises the question of whether the state, in designing its curriculum, can insist that the children who do attend the public schools learn the skills that the state believes are necessary for future citizens. The plaintiffs are saying no. They want to opt out of a portion of the curriculum, namely the reading curriculum. The state is saying that it can't achieve its goals unless it can teach critical reading and other skills in the reading program to all of the students attending the public schools.

If the plaintiffs' children continue to attend public school but do not participate in the reading curriculum, it would seem that the entire responsibility for teaching these children how to read would rest with the parents. What if these parents are incapable of teaching reading? Would anyone supervise them, or would they just blunder along?

In order to answer that, we have to step back. Tennessee has gone very far down the road of not supervising religious schools or home education. A lot of states don't permit home education because they don't believe it can match the rigorous curriculum that we have in the schools. But Tennessee decided to deal with the problem of religious objections to the public school curriculum by allowing parents to educate their children at home. The only real requirement is that the parents have a high school diploma and that the students pass some standardized tests.

What the district court did in the Mozert case was say that if you are going to allow parents to take their children out for the whole school day, you must also allow for the children to go to school for only part of the day. In other words, the ruling gives parents the right to shop around in the public school curriculum. This is what causes the problem. The state is essentially saying that if it is going to run a school system, it wants to be able to run it in such a way that the state's educational goals are met, and the court's decision doesn't permit this.

What sort of arguments are you making on behalf of the defendants?

We are not challenging the sincerity of the plaintiffs' religious beliefs, nor are we challenging their contention that the reading curriculum offends their religious beliefs. We are making two basic arguments. We are arguing that you can't have a violation of the free exercise clause unless religious beliefs are burdened. Since Tennessee allows parents to send their children to religious schools or educate them at home, there is no burden in requiring that the people who use the public schools accept the curriculum that the state has prescribed. The second argument is that even if there were a burden on the free exercise rights, there is no violation of the free exercise clause because there is a compelling state interest in maintaining the public school curriculum the way it is, and there is no less restrictive alternative means by which the state's interest can be achieved.

One component of this second argument has to do with the difficulty of having children come in and out of the class depending on whether their parents agree with the particular material that is being taught. This is especially difficult in grades one through four, where a single teacher meets with a class for the entire school day. In these grades, reading may be taught in one session in the morning, but the discussion of the reading material isn't confined to that one period. Students may well say something about what they read at any point during the day. What the court's decree means is that the teacher will have to monitor class discussions, and each time objectionable material comes up, she will have to say, "Just a moment. Johnny objects to what is being discussed here. I'm going to have to stop this discussion or send Johnny to the cafeteria." This would cause a serious disruption.

You can't understand what a serious problem this would cause unless you understand how sweeping the plaintiffs' beliefs are. The plaintiffs just don't like critical thinking skills. They want their children to be instructed that there is a right and a wrong and that's the end of it. Critical thinking requires that you appreciate opposing points of view, that you confront moral dilemmas, and that you be willing to discuss controversial issues. The plaintiffs don't want their children to have that kind of experience. They don't want their children to discuss anything that has religious implications unless the message is that their religious views are correct.

Can you provide some examples of issues that they see as having religious implications?

They believe that a wide variety of issues have such implications. Many topics that most of us would view as being secular, such as sex roles, environmental problems, disarmament, gun control, and the free enterprise system, they view in a religious light. At the trial, one of the plaintiffs was asked what current public issues didn't have religious implications for her. She answered, in essence, "Sewers and water bonds."

Their religious objections go beyond these types of issues. They are also concerned about their children being taught to be imaginative or to share the feelings of others. Similarly, they don't want their children to role play. All of these things, they feel, are impermissible if they go beyond the bounds of scripture. In other words, we are not just talking about excusing a child occasionally from class; we are talking about excusing the children from the entire reading program.

Do you see any other problems with Judge Hull's decision?

Well, on top of everything else, the decision could easily lead to divisiveness in the classroom. Dr. Robert Coles, a noted psychiatrist, testified about the tensions that could be caused by the relief sought by the plaintiffs. It would separate children out according to religious beliefs, and this would lead to one group seeing the other group as abnormal or inferior.

What worries me the most, however, are the possible ramifications of this decision. This decision goes well beyond establishing a limited opt-out program for a few children in Hawkins County. This is viewed as a test case by both sides. Concerned Women for America, the conservative group that has lent support to the plaintiffs, called a press conference after the initial decision was handed down, and they said that this decision will put pressure on other school systems. They also said that the decision shouldn't just apply to the reading curriculum; it should also apply to other areas, such as the social sciences, so that anyone who has religious objections to part of the curriculum can opt out.

Have conservative organizations played major roles in the battles over textbooks?

Concerned Women for America and similar organizations have played a catalytic and significant role in these cases, and I think it's fair to wonder whether these cases would have gone as far as they have without their support. I think, though, that it's a mistake to say that these organizations are an indispensable ingredient in terms of bringing these sessions to court. Perhaps they have been indispensable in the first cases, but once the principle is established, other people won't need these organizations to sue. They probably won't even need to sue. They'd just need to say, "Here's the law. If you don't give up, we'll sue." And the school would likely buckle under.

How do you respond to the people who say you are using scare tactics in this case?

I'm not the only person who sees this case as being of major significance. There are many educational organizations which see this decision as a very substantial threat to the public schools. When you sit down and analyze the decision, you'll see that it doesn't apply to just one group of parents, or one school district, or even one state. Court rulings apply to everybody, not just the people who happen to be in court. So, to answer your question, we're not using scare tactics. We're dealing with a very real threat.

Bibliography

Burress, Lee and Edward B. Jenkinson. *The Students' Right to Know*. Urbana, Illinois: National Council of Teachers of English, 1982.

Clark, Elyse. "A Slow, Subtle Exercise in Censorship." *School Library Journal* (March 1986): 93–96.

Cohen, Barbara. "Censoring the Sources." *School Library Journal* (March 1986): 97–99.

Davis, James E., ed. *Dealing with Censorship*. Urbana, Ill.: National Council of Teachers of English, 1979.

Donelson, Ken. "Almost 13 Years of Book Protests . . . Now What?" *School Library Journal* (March 1985): 93–98.

Goldberger, Judith M. "Judy Blume: Target of the Censor." *Newsletter on Intellectual Freedom* (May 1981).

Hentoff, Nat. *The First Freedom: The Tumultuous History of Free Speech in America*. New York: Namar, 1980.

Jenkinson, Edward B. *Censors in the Classroom: The Mind Benders*. Carbondale, Ill.: Southern Illinois University Press, 1979.

Klein, Norma. "Being Banned." *Top of the News* 34 (Spring 1985): 248–255.

176 TRUST YOUR CHILDREN

Klein, Norma. "Some Thoughts on Censorship: An Author Symposium." *Top of the News* 32 (Winter 1983): 137–153.

McClure, Amy. "Intellectual Freedom and the Young Child." *Children's Literature Association Quarterly* 8 (Fall 1983): 41–43.

McClure, Amy. "Limiting the Right to Choose: Censorship of Children's Reading." *Children's Literature Association Quarterly* 7 (Spring 1982): 39–42.

Musser, Louise S. "Censoring Sexist and Racist Books: Unjustified and Unjust." *Children's Literature Association Quarterly* 9 (Spring 1984): 36–37.

Parker, Barbara and Stefanie Weiss. *Protecting the Freedom to Learn: A Citizen's Guide.* Washington, D.C.: People for the American Way, 1983.

Peck, Richard. "The Genteel Unshelving of a Book." *School Library Journal* (May 1986): 37–39.

Ranta, Taimi. "Huck Finn and Censorship." *Children's Literature Association Quarterly* 8 (Winter 1983): 35.

Tucker, Nicholas, ed. *Suitable for Children? Controversies in Children's Literature.* Berkeley: University of California Press, 1976.

Zettner, Pat. "A Perfect Day for Broccoli Spears: Learning the Way through the Never-Never Land of Textbook Taboos." *Writer's Digest* (April 1986): 70–72.

Zuckerman, Linda. "A Publisher's Perspective." *Horn Book Magazine* (Sept.–Oct. 1986): 629–633.